# PSIl

# GROWING BIBLE

*The Complete Psilocybin Mushroom Cultivation Guide. Step by Step to Grow Indoor and Outdoor Your Magic Psychedelic Mushrooms with Safety Measure.*

## By Tyler Barrett

# Disclaimer

All Erudition contained in this book is given for informational and educational purposes only. The author is not in any way accountable for any results or outcomes that emanate from using this material. Constructive attempts have been made to provide information that is both accurate and effective, but the author is not bound for the accuracy or use/misuse of information.

# Foreword

First, I will like to thank you for taking the first step of trusting me and deciding to purchase/read this life transforming eBook. Thanks for spending your time and resources on this material. I can assure you of exact blueprint I lay bare in the information manual you are currently reading. It has transformed lives, and I strongly believe it will equally transform your life too. All the information I presented in this Do-It-Yourself is easy to digest and practice.

# Contents

# CHAPTER 1

## *Where to grow your mushroom*

**O**utdoor cultivation

Growing outdoor mushrooms are ideal in many ways because the forest (or any dreary area with good humidity and air flow) provides the perfect fruiting conditions without the need of the farmer for any climate control. In fact, the forest is where the mushrooms we grow come from, so why not just grow them out there? This is the thought which led to the development of Cornell's initial mushroom research and extension project led by Professor Kenneth Mudge (now Emeritus), who was particularly interested in agroforestry, or the combination of trees, forests, and crop production.

Ken has been studying many species for nearly 15 years, mainly concentrating on log-grown shiitake mushrooms as they quickly proved to have the most economical viability. We also know that mane, oyster, wine cap Stropharia can be successfully grown outdoors, and a few other minor species. The main restriction with outdoor or forest cultivation is that only the log-grown shiitake can grow consistently enough out of the species mentioned above to produce weekly mushrooms, a necessary part of the supply chain to a farm company. This is due to the unique property that shiitake logs can be soaked or "forced" into fruit by immersing the logs in water for 12-24 hours, which encourages them to bear fruit. This process can be used to grow relatively consistently mushrooms from around the first week of June through the middle to late part of October, at least in Central New York's climate. Although efficient, the other species produce fruit on their own, and so are not good choices if the goal is to yield consistent market yields.

### Indoor Growing

Once we step out of the woods and into an enclosed space, the list of species that we can reliably grow begins to expand considerably. In addition, we must also begin to monitor and maintain the ideal environment for the different production stages, from incubation to fruiting. And probably the most challenging thing, we need to take extra measures to reduce and eliminate contamination sources in our substrates, which will arrest and prevent fruiting of our desired mushrooms. With outdoor production, this issue is almost non-existent, a big advantage point. Indoor farming systems are sometimes called "controlled agricultural environment," which includes other systems such as hydroponics, aquaponics, and greenhouse production. Unlike CEA systems used for greens and herbs, mushrooms can be produced in locations with limited infrastructure and resources for production start-up and sustainability. However, considerations and controls need to be made regarding the present temperature, humidity, light, and airflow.

A major advantage of indoor manufacturing is that systems can be adapted to work in a wide range of abandoned and underused farm infrastructure including barns, outbuildings, high tunnels, and storage. The basements, shipping containers and warehouse spaces can easily be retrofitted for production in an urban environment. This positions mushrooms as a system accessible for both rural and urban farms, as well as those farmers with limited capital and access to other start-up resources.

# CHAPTER 2

## *Sterile culture technique*

**M**ushroom food (properly known as its substratum) is much like human food: a nutritious mixture that contains a balance of carbohydrates, proteins, minerals, and vitamins. Like our food too, I find a variety of microorganisms quite delightful, as a loaf of bread left out in the kitchen counter will quickly prove for more than a few days. Unlike humans, however, fungi are also micro-organisms and must compete with any other neighborhood micro-organisms for food. Bacteria and molds have a competitive edge because they can reproduce thousands, even millions of times faster than the average species of mushrooms can. Any substrate that even contains a single mold spore or bacterium will likely end up a moldy or mushy mess. Furthermore, in the average room, the average cubic centimeter of air contains more than 100,000 particles. No matter how scrupulously clean you think it is, an invisible, silent rain of mold spores, dust particles, and pollen grains settles constantly on every horizontal surface in your home. The only way to prevent these critics from hijacking the mushroom cultures is to ensure that they never get on to them first. There are two general ways to do this: by working in a truly clean (i.e., sterile) environment, they thoroughly kill whatever molds or bacteria are there, to begin with, and exclude any other. We extract pollutants from our products by sterilizing them in a pressure cooker, where practically no living thing may withstand the high temperatures (1210 C/ 255' F) and pressures (15 psi) within them. We then create a sterile working environment by filtering the air in our workspace and/or using chemical disinfectants to sterilize it.

Those two techniques constitute the technique of sterile or aseptic farming, which is by far the most important thing you need to know to succeed in cultivating the mushrooms. Let me reiterate this for emphasis: The most important thing you can learn from this book is the sterile culture technique. If you do not figure out this one, none of the methods of cultivation will work, no matter how closely you follow the instructions. If you're really, really lucky, you might harvest one or two mushrooms, but mostly you'll have a gleaming array of blue, green, and black molds and a slimy, stinky bacteria collection. Many would-be mushroom growers have failed right here, and those who succeeded (including your humble authors) have learned the hard way of using sterile culture techniques and why. It is our hope that the strategies presented in this chapter will show you the easy way, saving you time and heartbreak.

### Cleaning your work area

The preparation of a clean workspace is the first task. Ideally, you can only dedicate a room or space to your mushroom projects, like a spare bedroom or an unused walk-in closet. If there is no such space, then much of the laboratory work can be accomplished in an average kitchen, but this requires you to establish and maintain a pristine level of cleanliness. The kitchen competes with the bathroom as the house's messiest and biologically active room, and the counts of molds there tend to be very high. Working in a kitchen, on the other hand, provides convenient access to a water source and furnace top. If you're planning to devote a separate space to mushrooming, make sure it's near the kitchen. There's no point in sterilizing your materials just to carry them into your laboratory through a dirty house. A good-sized table should be in the workspace, preferably one with a continuous, easily cleaned upper surface. Formica or enamel is ideal because before each use you will need to wipe the workbench with alcohol. If you have a wooden table, consider putting on top of it a piece of thin plywood with a plastic laminate surface, or a piece of heavy, thick vinyl when working. Similarly, it should be easy to clean the workspace floor (linoleum or tile), and easy to inspect for cleanliness. Carpets are spores and dust repositories, millions of which are kicked into the air every step of the way and should be avoided if possible. The walls must be clean (a fresh coat of paint wouldn't hurt), and any other room spaces and surfaces should be cleaned thoroughly. Use a solution for disinfecting if practical (orange-oil based products are good as they are mild but effective biocides and environmentally friendly). Obviously, if you work in your kitchen, you can't disinfect every surface whenever you plan to use it, but you should still give it a regular deep cleaning and disinfect as much of it as you can before every use. Space should be void of drafts to minimize air circulation around your cultures. Windows should be tightly closed, heating or air-conditioning ducts should be covered, and doors should be closed long before you start work. Whenever possible eliminate other sources of contamination from the room. Potted plants, fish tanks, food plates for pets, litter boxes: get them all out of there. It is helpful to run an air-filtration device in the space too.

Good ones nowadays cost less than $100 and are silent and efficient enough to run continuously. Make sure the unit you are buying is rated HEF'A. HEPA stands for Particulate Air with high efficiency. It is an official filter rating which means it captures 0.1 microns (1/100th of a millimeter) and larger particles, or 99. 97 percent of airborne solid matter. So, give the air in the room a thorough scrubbing, we keep our filter on low at all times and run it up for at least an hour before working in the lab. Finally, in your immediate work area, you need to clean the air. This can be done by working inside a glove box, an enclosed space that can be thoroughly disinfected and is draft-free, or in front of a flow hood, a large

HEPA filter unit that blows a steady stream of pure sterile air over your workspace, excluding all contaminants. A glove box can be quickly and inexpensively installed but is less effective because the air from the space can find its way inside.

## Personal Hygiene

Now that your space has been cleaned and prepared, it's time to consider the other primary source of contamination in your makeshift laboratory: you. Your hair, body, and clothes are an Amazon jungle of bacteria, viruses, and fungi that are all invisible to your eyes, mostly harmless to you or others, but deadly to the mushroom cultures. You should be as neat as possible before each work session to keep that nasty horde to a minimum. That means showering, drying off with a freshly laundered towel and dressing immediately before working in a clean set of clothes. It's also important to choose your clothing; don't wear long-sleeved shirts or loose-fitting items that might flop around while you work. If you've got long hair, tie it up on your head. Use isopropyl (rubbing) alcohol, wash your hands and lower arms and always wear disposable surgical gloves when operating (wipe the outside of the gloves too, use alcohol).

## Mental Hygiene

Just as you've packed your workspace and body, make sure you're still taking care of your state of mind before working. Mental hygiene is as critical as personal hygiene because the way you work will be affected by your state of mind, and if you are disturbed or rushed, you are likely to make mistakes or contaminate your culture. Your laboratory movements should be systematic, calculated and deliberate. Avoid unnecessary fast or jerky movements, as they produce only unwanted air currents. Take your moment. If you're hurried, slow down or save the idea for a day you've got more time. In the same way, ask your partner, kids, dog or cat not to enter the room or interrupt you while you are working and disconnecting your phone. Play calming, elevating music if you like, but avoid Stockhausen or speed metal, unless you find it to your ears to relax.

# CHAPTER 3

## *Equipment and supplies*

Mushroom cultivation requires equipment, including many specific devices. A couple of these items are explicit to the point that they must be bought from mushroom cultivation supply houses, however, most can without much of a stretch be found at I an assortment of neighborhood sources. A significant number of the materials you need fire likewise sold for some other, increasingly mundane reason; while making shopping simpler, this has the additional advantage of giving good spread to those, wishing to stay under the radar on their cultivation activities. Home improvement shops, kitchen, and café supply houses, pet stores, home fermenting providers, and garden focuses are the fortune troves of the stealthy (or simply economical) mushroom cultivator. Whenever conceivable, we have attempted to give numerous general sources to every one of the items you may require.

## Equipment

### Pressure Cooker

This will be one of the most utilized items in your cultivation apparatus shed, so it is important to get a better than average one right from the start. Since you will use it to disinfect generally large items, and in quantity, size is basic. If you can manage the cost of a larger unit than you at first need, get it, since you will likely need to update later anyway. The key determinant for what size you ought to get is the number of quart jars you can securely clean at once. Since bricklayer jars are unpredictably shaped, generally few can fit easily inside even the largest pressure cooker, constraining the measure of material you can process at once. In this manner, we recommend getting a unit that can hold at least seven-quart jars without a moment's delay; the model we use, the All American #941, holds more than twice that many.

There are various options as to what brand and type to get, yet one stands apart from the group: The All-American brand, manufactured by the Aluminum Foundry of Wisconsin. All American pressure cookers are the best-made, generally reliable, and accessible to the safest. The company has been doing business for a long time, and since they were first introduced, the design of their pressure cookers has not fundamentally changed. They're made primarily of overwhelming test cast aluminum, and they don't have elastic seals or wear-out sections. Replacement parts are readily accessible, and even a 20-year-old unit purchased at a secondhand shop or on eBay can be made to work well as new.

Like smaller, lower-priced kitchen pressure cookers, all Americans have a huge, extremely accurate dial scale that lacks a method of determining the internal pressure decisively. They are also intended to hold a vacuum after cooling which is necessary to prevent the existence of non-sterile air in your crops.

There are two general types of pressure cookers to choose from: those with or similar to a vapor discharge valve, and those with a metal-weighted "rocker" that releases steam at any point above a certain pressure level. The last sort should be prevented, if possible, as this rapid arrival of pressure would cause the fluids inside the cooker to boil over, dramatically demolishing the media and wrecking. Pressure cookers can be used in rocker style, but they need increasingly rigorous monitoring during use to avoid these accidents. (Each American makes the two types; the type of stopcock they call pressure "sterilizers," while the weighted rockers are known as pressure "canners.") Whatever brand and model of pressure cooker you choose, make sure it's in good working order and you understand its operation and well-being (i.e., read the manual). Make sure all seals and gaskets match like a fiddle, and the cover bolts to the frame tightly. There should be no steam escaping around the seals once it is pressurized. Turn off the heat source, allow the cooker to cool down completely, and properly reseat the top if there is one. Running a Vaseline dot around the edge of cookers in metal-on-metal design will ensure a tight fit and help shield the cover from seizure to base during use. Before each usage make sure you add a suitable measure of water to the bottom of the cooker, in any case, adequate to bring the depth to 1/2 inch. Never position items directly at the bottom of the pressure cooker, or allow them to touch the outer dividers, where temperatures are highest.

Most pressure cookers are supported by a rack or trivet intended to hold the contents over the water surface and the larger All-American models have basket-shaped liners to prevent products from direct contact with the cooker itself. Let the pressure cooker slowly begin to come up to temperature. Excessively quick or lopsided heating can cause containers to burst or crack. Until closing the stopcock, always bring the cooker to a full head of steam to displace cooler air pockets. That may take a moment, particularly on larger cookers. Before shutting the door, you should see a strong flux of steam coming from the stopcock tube. Never leave unattended an under-pressure cooker. The pressure and temperature inside a cooker can change unpredictably, particularly during the initial heating periods, before the cooker still doesn't seem to be leveling fully. It is important that the cooker remain at the ideal pressure for the full cycle in order to prevent a blast and guarantee complete sanitization. Check it at regular intervals or so to ensure it is not under-or overheating and vary the source of heat. Just allow the cooker to cool slowly and all by itself. Never touch the outside of the cooker when pressurized, and do not use cold water to cool it even faster. This can cause the cooker to implode and its contents to discharge savagely. It will generate a large measure of risky energy, at any rate. Wrap an alcohol-splashed paper towel around the valve before venting it to release any residual pressure to prevent unsterile air from being drawn into the pressure cooker upon opening. Pressure cookers are potentially dangerous things. They produce high temperatures and vapor that can cause injury. Like a very sharp blade, a pressure cooker is an apparatus that demands consideration and alertness and consequently gives a great advantage.

### Petri Dishes

Petri dishes are shallow, transparent plastic or glass dishes with a baggy spread. They arrive in a variety of sizes, yet the most useful size for parasitic cultures is 100 x 15 mm. Reusable glass or Pyrex dishes are long enduring and autoclavable yet are generally costly. Pre-sterilized dispensable polystyrene dishes come in sleeves of 20 or 25. They are practical, yet since they are intended to be used just once and afterward discarded, they aren't actually earth cordial. The two types of Petri dishes can be re-sterilized utilizing hydrogen peroxide and a microwave:

1.  Wash the plates altogether with dishwashing cleanser, taking unique care to totally expel any residual agar.

2.  Pour a small measure of 3% peroxide into each dish and whirl it around to open it to the whole

inside surface of the plate. Repeat with its spread and place it on the dish.

3. Put the pile of dishes in the microwave and heat at medium force until all the peroxide has been powered off on the plates.

4. Immediately use the plates or place them in a perfect plastic bag until appropriate.

This technique is ideally paired with the use of peroxide in cultivations of agar. Use pre-sterilized plastic or autoclaved glass dishes is safer when working with agar which lacks peroxide. We recommend the addition of hydrogen peroxide to your cultures at any point imaginable to reduce sullying and allow you to work with agar in a not exactly perfect condition.

In any case, peroxide, for example, cannot be used in specific circumstances when producing spores. In these cases, we find that plaques with a diameter of 50 mm are easier to keep clean, due to their reduced surface area. You can use 4-ounce jam jars or similar heatproof glass containers if the Petri dishes are unavailable. They have the advantage to be reusable but lack clear lids and take up more than twice as much space as plates for the community.

### Media Flasks

Media flasks are used for holding fluid media during sanitization and pouring Petri plates. Any thick-walled, autoclavable glass jug will do, however, attempt to find one with a generally restricted neck to encourage pouring. One and a half-liter squeezed apple or shimmering water bottles with screw top caps are ideal for this reason.

### Mason Jars

We use standard Ball-style mason canning jars, generally in quart sizes. They are readily accessible, strong, and can be reused uncertainly. For grain spawn, limited mouth (70 mm) quart jars are ideal. In the event that you need to attempt the so-called "PF" method, you'll need straight-sided, half-16 ounces jam jars.

A note of alert: mason jars are solid; however, they do sometimes break. Always review them intently before use for cracks, dispose of suspicious-looking ones immediately, and be extra careful when shaking jars of grain. Don't smack them down onto the palm of your hand to separate the grains; a cracked jar can take a finger directly off. Instead, simply hold the jar by the lid end and shake it here and there. In the event that the grain is really firmly bound, and you should break it up persuasively, carefully hit the jar against a spotless towel supported by a thick cushion or against a halfway used move of pipe tape until it slackens up. (Make sure that the lid is firmly fixed too; you don't need your precious spawn flying all over the place.) Always permit your pressure cooker to heat up steadily; fast heating can cause jars to crack because of the temperature distinction between their insides and outsides.

### Mason Jar Lids

Don't mess with the metal lids given in two pieces; spare those for canned tomatoes. We use a one-piece plastic lid for culture work, which is heat-resistant and modified easily to allow the legal exchange of gas. The ball makes a "Stockpiling Cap" plastic. Even though the bundling notes that these caps are "not for storage," they are simply autoclavable. You will carefully bore or cut an I-inch gap in the focal point of each cap to alter those lids. When fitted with a filter circle (see next section), these modified caps enable gasses (not yet contaminants) to go through the jar all over, so that your cultures can breathe freely.

### Filter Disks

Placed between the lid and the jar's mouth, filter plates allow the exchange of gases without contaminants being exposed. They are made of a heat resistant synthetic fiber and can be regularly sterilized. They are a couple of millimeters thick and come pre-cut to match the correct jar-and-lid mix. Occasionally, when in contact with soil or form spores, they discolor. In that case, simply drill them on a medium-term basis in a 1/4-quality fade arrangement (i.e., 1/4-CUP standard quality dye in 3/4-Cup water) unlike these plates, an affordable option is Tyvek, which can be cut to fit over the jar lid. Tyvek is a synthetic material that is used in a range of applications.

Building supply stores will purchase rolls, and smaller quantities are available to Ups or the U.S. for nothing. Mail station like those oversized, indestructible envelopes for mailing. Beca using Tyvek is thinner and more flexible than the business filter plates, it should be cut more deeply around and around than the jarhead, and one inch will hang off the edge of the jar. Tyvek is also reusable but should be discarded after three or four applications.

## Spawn Bags

Otherwise known as filter repair bags, these are transparent, heat-resistant, gusseted flexible plastic bags used to hold large spawning amounts. They are autoclavable and have on one side a small square filter for exchanging air. They are stacked with soil, sterilized, immunized, and fixed with an impulse (heat) sealer afterward. They are suitable for growing out large quantities of spawn because they are versatile, and it is possible to control or analyze the interior contents for pollutants without effort. They lose their heating versatility and are generally good for solitary use only, but bags fit as a fiddle can be completely cleaned out and sterilized again.

We've seen farmers use "oven bags" (or spawns) in the grocery store. While these are autoclavable and can be made to work, they lack a filter repair that doesn't exactly provide an ideal exchange of gas, and they're too small to even think about seal heating. One way to equip this sort of bag with some breathability is to wrap its neck tightly around a thick wad of polyfill or cotton and seal it firmly with a significant breathability

## Impulse Sealer

Impulse sealers are used for fixing spawn bags. Make certain to get one wide enough to straddle the whole bag when extended flat, at any rate, 12 inches across. E-Bay is a good place to search for bargains on impulse sealers.

### Alcohol Lamp

This is a glass lamp with a cotton wick and metal neckline. Loaded up with scouring alcohol, it gives a spotless fire to disinfecting surgical tools and inoculation loops as you work.

Then again, you can use a:

### Mini torch

Sold in kitchen supply houses for caramelizing the outside layer on creme Brule, and sold in gadgets stores for soldering, these smaller than usual butane lights are useful for disinfecting tools as you work. A good quality one will have a solid base to keep it upstanding while it sits on the seat top.

### Balance

Mechanical or electronic models are similarly good. The important characteristics to search for in a balance are precision to in any event 0.5 g, the ability to weigh up to at least 250 g (1 kg is better) and a dish sufficiently large to suit oversized items.

### Surgical blade

Surgical blades are used for cutting and moving agar and tissue cultures. A thin-handled dismembering surgical tool with dispensable #10-sized sharp edges is ideal. If you can't find these, an all-aluminum Xacto-style blade will work OK, however, it tends to be to some degree harder to move into tight spaces.

### Inoculation Loop

This wire loop toward the end of a metal or wooden handle is used to move spores or small measures of mycelium to agar plates. It very well may be found in logical or brew making supply stores or made from a dowel and a bit of thin solid wire. An inoculation loop isn't required in the event that you use the "cardboard circle" method of spore germination.

### Sharpies

This perpetual compose anyplace markers are essential for naming culture containers of all kind.

### Pipes

It is useful to have two types of plastic or metal channels: a thin necked one for pouring fluids and fine powders, and a wide-mouthed one for filling jars.

### Estimating [Serological] Pipette and Rubber Bulb

If you intend to work with agar, you'll need some way of estimating small volumes of fluid (1–15 mL) to add to your cultures. Ten-milliliter glass estimating pipettes are ideal for this purpose since they are autoclavable, reusable, and have markings on them to effortlessly determine volume. An elastic bulb is used to draw and administer fluids from the pipette. Both can be found at logical providers and some home mix stores. A glass 10-milliliter graduated chamber or a set of metal estimating spoons can be used for this purpose, however, it will require even more handling and care to avoid polluting your cultures while you work.

### Graduated Cylinders

These are used to accurately quantify fluids. Cylinders in 1-liter, 1 OO-milliliter, and 10-milliliter sizes should consider every contingency.

### Measuring cups and spoons

Measuring cups and spoons can be used in place of graduated tubes but are less precise to some degree. For 1-cup (250rnl) to 8-cup (2 L) numbers, use Pyrex ones, and for smaller amounts use metal ones. Where sterility is needed before use, the two types can be autoclaved or sterilized in boiling water (5 minutes at a moving boil).

### Syringes

Syringes are used to do mass inoculation in spore, a system called "Psilocybe Fanaticus." Ten-or twenty-milliliter sizes are used, including large bore needles (18-measure). In a pressure cooker, they may be autoclaved twice, or sterilized in boiling water. From cautious and veterinary retail shops, and from some online vendors of mushroom supplies, syringes can be purchased.

In any event, their contract is regulated in various U.S. states, and they can be elusive locally at times. When you buy spore syringes pre-filled, after use, clean and spare the syringe and needle. They are autoclavable and normally reusable.

### Supplies

### Hydrogen Peroxide (3%)

This antiseptic is added to cultures to shield them from defilement. It is accessible at most pharmacies or grocery stores. The real convergence of hydrogen peroxide arrangements sometimes fluctuates, so make sure the date on the bottle is of late vintage (See sidebar underneath for a method of finding hydrogen peroxide's focus level). Right now, is generally harmless to human health and requires no unique handling methods, besides wearing gloves. It is a mellow fading operator, so be careful not to dribble it onto clothing.

Increasingly concentrated (8–35%) arrangements are accessible from a variety of sources, for example, pool supply stores, and on the web. Hydrogen peroxide in focuses greater than 3% can cause severe consumes and is potentially combustible, so be careful when working with it. Peroxide corrupts reasonably quickly, to protect that it stays at the correct focus, use the bottle at the earliest opportunity subsequent to opening. Between uses, envelop the neck and cap by parafilm or plastic wrap, and store the bottle inside a spotless plastic bag in the cooler. Prior to each use, wipe down the outside of the bottle and cap (counting the mouth and neck beneath the cap) with alcohol, and take uncommon care not to touch any piece of the bottle itself with your hands or tools while apportioning. Always sanitize pipettes and graduated cylinders that will come into contact with peroxide before use, either in a pressure cooker along with your media or by submerging them in boiling water for 5 minutes.

### Isopropyl [Rubbing) Alcohol

This is used for sanitizing hands, surfaces and containers, and as fuel for alcohol lamps. It is accessible in grocery stores and pharmacies in either 70% or 91 % focuses, both of which is reasonable. Cautioning: Isopropanol is profoundly combustible!! Get it far from open blazes, if you don't mind make sure whatever alcohol you have used has completely evaporated before you light your alcohol lamp.

### Blanch

Standard quality laundry dye is useful for cleaning surfaces and tools. Avoid brands with added cleansers. Weaken to in any event 1/4 quality before use. A 10% quality arrangement in a spray bottle is an excellent surface and air disinfectant.

### Parafilm

Parafilm is a paraffin-based, flexible film utilized to seal Petri dishes. It is gas permeable, which means that it takes into account gas exchange while keeping contaminants out of cultures. An advantageous form in 1-inchwide rolls is sold by some garden supply vendors as "Uniting Tape." If you can't find Parafilm, you can substitute polyethylene stick film, for example, Glad Wrap (yet not Saran Wrap or similar brands, which are made from polyvinylchloride and are not gas permeable.). Utilizing a sharp blade, carefully cut a 1-to 2-inch-wide segment off the end of a full roll.

### Surgical Gloves

Dispensable latex gloves are essential for getting grimy hands far from your perfect cultures. They need not be pre-sterilized. Simply wash your hands and arms a long time before putting them on, at that point wipe the outside of the gloves with an alcohol-drenched paper towel (always permit them to dry totally before going anyplace close to an open fire.)

### Substrates & Casing Materials

### Whole Grains

For spawn creation, the most commonly used substrate is entire grain. Entire grains make an ideal mechanism for spawn for a number of reasons. Each grain demonstrations like a smaller than normal capsule of supplements, minerals, and water that is handily colonized by higher fungi, while its sinewy husk halfway shields it from contamination by different living beings. Upon colonization, the grains are effectively separated from each other. At long last, when colonized grain spawn is used to immunize mass substrates, each grain fills in as a minimal container of mycelium and supplement holds, a remote station from which the fungus can leap off onto the new medium.

While practically any cereal grain will work as spawn, we recommend delicate winter (white) wheat, since it has worked well for us, and is by all accounts liberated from the bacterial contaminants that can be present on rye and different grains. You may use whatever grains are readily accessible to u, however we do suggest utilizing larger bit grains like rye, wheat, or corn, instead of small-grained cereals like millet or rice, which tend to cluster together when cooked. We have seen a few growers use wild birdseed mix with good results, which has the undeniable bit of leeway of being modest and readily accessible. Be that as it may, because it is a mixture of various sized grains, birdseed is increasingly difficult to moisten appropriately. It can likewise be very clingy when damp. To limit these issues, hydrate birdseed with a 24-hour cold soak instead of boiling water, and flush and drain it very well before stacking into containers. You should attempt to use natural grains at whatever point conceivable, since that is the best way to guarantee that they have not been treated with fungicides.

### Malt Extract, Dried

This is a powdered extract of grains that have been "malted" or developed to advance the incomplete transformation of their starch into sugars. Malt extract is used as an important substitute in agar products. It is readily accessible from preparing suppliers. Make sure to use light or tan malt. Darker malts have been caramelized and fungi are not growing well on caramelized sugars.

### Yeast Extract

A dried extract of yeast cells, plentiful in vitamins, minerals, and protein, yeast extract is added to agar media as a wholesome enhancement. Brewer's yeast, accessible in numerous health food stores, is an adequate substitute, however it isn't as effective as evident yeast extract.

### Calcium Carbonate [CaCo3)

Calcium carbonate is otherwise called lime, hydrated lime, limestone flour, clam shell flour, and chalk. It is used to cradle the pH of packaging soils and substrates, demoralize contamination, and give calcium to the growing fungus. Fungi tend to prefer slightly fundamental (for example pH > 8) media, while microbes and some different contaminants don't. Check the name to be certain the calcium carbonate you buy is low in magnesium « 1 %), because a few fungi don't grow well on substrates containing high measures of it.

### Calcium Sulfate

Also called gypsum, calcium sulfate is used to capture overabundance water in substrates, making them simpler to shake or separate, and assisting with preventing water logging and contamination. It is essentially impartial in pH and has no buffering capability.

### Hardwood Sawdust and Chips

These are substrates for the genus Psilocybe cyanescens, P. azurescens and related lignicolous species (wood-possessing). Birch, cottonwood, oak, birch, and beech are suitable, though most hardwood species will do so. In case you have any of these tree species growing nearby, you might have the option to get fresh chips from your nearby highway office or garden focus, or you might be able to chip your own. Chips developed in winter or late winter from trees are best as they will be highest in sugars and contain at least green matter, which can be a contamination vector in beds.

You can sometimes get local hardwood chips from grill vendors, who market them for use in food smokers. If you don't tackle hardwoods locally, you can buy wood chips online. Fine chipped wood beech or maple chips are marketed as creature bedding (Beta-Chip and SaniChip are two brands to pay special attention to), yet they are usually too fine to even suggest using alone, and need to be paired with larger chips or something to affect them.

### Sawdust Fuel Pellets

Used for home heating in special wood stoves, these are made from sawdust compressed into tiny pellets. During production, the high heat generated: makes them pretty sterile. The pellets fall into sawdust once more when they are moistened with warm water. This item is available at home heating suppliers as well as some home improvement stores. Stove pellets make a good source of sawdust for substrates–just make sure to get a brand made from hardwoods only. In a number of tree species, including birch and oak, they are additionally sold as fuel to food smokers.

### Spiral-Grooved Dowels

Spiral-grooved dowels are readily accessible from woodworking providers as furniture-joining pegs; the best ones for mushroom use are 1 to 2 inches long and 1/4-inch or 5/16-inch in diameter. They are normally made from birch and will be assigned thusly. They are most commonly utilized in mushroom cultivation on logs, where the colonized pegs are beat into openings around the perimeter of the log. The spiral furrow around the outside of the peg gives a maximal surface area from which the mycelium can leap off onto resulting substrates.

### Paper Pellet Cat Litter

Used for the capacity of cultures in small glass tubes. The free, open structure and restricted nourishing content of paper makes it ideal for the long-term maintenance of most mushroom species. Search for a brand that is unscented and made of 100% reused paper; Crown, Good Mews, and Yesterday's News are three brands we have found to be effective.

### Peat Moss

A component of casing soil, peat moss is sold in garden focuses all over the place. While it has minimal healthy benefit, its high-water holding capacity gives dampness to the creating fruitbodies. It is to some degree acidic and must be cradled with calcium carbonate.

### Vermiculite

Vermiculite is another component of casing soil. It is used for its water holding capacity, and its soft, open structure, which permits appropriate gas exchange. It is accessible at many garden providers. Use the coarsest grade you can find. There is a fantasy that vermiculite contains asbestos, which isn't valid. Apparently, there was a solitary vermiculite mine in Montana that was debased with asbestos, and it was closed. After this episode was publish moss and vermiculite. Different manufacturers started testing their vermiculite for asbestos, yet it was not found anyplace else. In any case, vermiculite and similar materials (like peat and calcium salts) do contain a great deal of extremely fine particulates, which can be harmful whenever breathed in. Always wear a painter's residue veil when handling them in their dry state.

## Water Crystals

Made from a synthetic polymer chemically similar to super paste, these crystals can maintain their weight in water by 400 times, and then slowly discharge it back into their atmosphere. We feel like smooth gelatin when fully hydrated. These are used to track water use in agriculture and gardening and to prevent plants from drying out completely between watering. These are added to the casing soil in mushroom cultivation to help maintain sufficient levels of humidity. The crystals come in two assortments: the ones made from potassium sodium or others. Since elevated sodium levels are harmful to multiple fungi, make sure to get the potassium-made version. (One brand based on potassium is called "Land Sorb").

## Spores

Obviously, none of any of these materials are of any use to you in the event that you don't have mushroom spores to grow on them. Why at that point, you ask, didn't we disclose to you first where to get your hands on some Psilocybe spores?

It's a good inquiry, and one that requires an entangled answer, tragically. Almost certainly you live in a country that has (anyway strange the notion) regarded these unassuming and delicate mushrooms illegal. While the specialists can do little to genuinely contain these life forms (no more so than if they somehow managed to boycott the shape growing on your shower drapery), they could detain you for horsing around with them. That is a pitiful truth worth contemplating for a moment before you choose to do as such. If, at last, you conclude that the prizes exceed the risks (as we accept, they do), we ask you to practice alert while doing a/1ything unlawful. Stay under the radar; be prudent. Don't converse with others about your new hobby (or if nothing else not except if you know for total sure they are "cool"). Think of conceivable elective implications for your buys, regardless of whether you just instruct them to yourself: the 50-pound bag of w) 1eat berries is to crush your own bread flour, the malt is for your next clump of home brewed chocolate watchman, etc. Don't gloat about your endeavors on the Internet; anyway, mysterious you think you are anything you do online nowadays can be followed back to your PC, if somebody needed to. It may require a court request, however it's despite everything better not to face the challenge. Do not begin this hobby with the notion that instantly you'll turn into the neighborhood psychedelic mushroom boss, a parasitic Tony Montana. The benefit thought process has driven endless individuals adrift, as it might you be able to.

# CHAPTER 4

## *PF TEK Improved*

I n this chapter, along with our refinements of it, we describe the popular "Psilocybe Fanaticus" mushroom cultivation technique, otherwise known as the "PF Tek." This method is the first system to be exposed to for many Psilocybe mushroom growers nowadays, so we felt it was important that we cover it in our book, even if we don't recognize it as a general practice. Since it is as similar to foolproof as a method of growing mushrooms can get, it is a good starting point for a beginner. It requires a minimum investment of time and expense, and in a relatively short time exposes the novice to the whole life cycle of a mushroom. Taking a close and first-hand look at this process will allow you to understand the principles that underlie the more complex procedures that follow. If you choose to start your mushroom cultivation with a Psilocybe cubensis spore-water syringe rather than a spore print, this method is a good way to use it (although not the only one: you could also use it to directly inoculate grain spawning. The technique allows you to very quickly produce a pure fruiting strain of P. cubensis, with minimal interference. Above this is placed a thin layer of dry vermiculite, followed by a few layers of aluminum foil. The brown rice flour provides the colonization of the fungus with a healthy nutrient base, while the vermiculite acts as a reservoir for water and helps create an open, airy structure that allows the growing crops to breathe. The jars are then sterilized in a pressure cooker or bath with boiling water. Upon cooling, the first layer of foil is removed, and at various points around the jar's diameter the jars are easily filled with a few milliliters of a spore solution from a syringe. The top layer of foil is replaced, and the jars are then placed in an incubator or a warm, draft-free spot. With time the spores will germinate and fuse to form a dikaryotic mycelium with an appropriate mate.

In each injection, the large number of spores ensures that mating will occur and that each jar contains a wide variety of strains. The many strains present are competing to colonize the jar, with the weaker ones being overtaken by the most vigorous (and by extension, most likely to well bear fruit). The jars should be completely colonized after some weeks or so and are ready to be fruited. The "cakes" of mycelium are knocked out of the jars at this point in the original PF Tek and placed upside down on a bed of moistened perlite at the bottom of a clear container such as an aquarium or a plastic storage bin, which is covered to maintain high humidity levels. The fruiting chamber is placed under a light source (fluorescent lights grow connected to a timer or even a brightly illuminated window). Once or twice a day, the cover is removed, and the cakes are fanned by hand to remove built-up $CO_2$, then misted with water from a hand spray bottle. In time, primordia form on the cake's outer surface and eventually ripen into full-sized mushrooms. We leave the substratum in the jar in our "improved" PF Tek, and mushrooms fruit only from the top surface of the jar. This serves a series of ends. One, it eliminates the need for perlite tubs which are elaborate and messy. Instead, the jars are perforated into any clear enclosed container, or even a plastic bag, to allow exchange of gas.

Second, the need for high ambient humidity is reduced, because the top layer of pure vermiculite acts as a casing layer, holding a reservoir of water that can be drawn from the developing fruits. Because fruiting is confined to a horizontal surface, the forming mushrooms retain a much more natural appearance and form. On the other hand, the original "cake" approach tends to produce fruits of odd shapes and sizes, as they grow around the cake at random points. (Since spores are most efficiently dispersed from downward-facing gills, most mushrooms utilize gravity to orient themselves horizontally. If, as in our method, the stipes are already pointing in the right direction, they naturally grow straight and tall.) By incorporating a casing layer, the "improved" PF Tek resembles more closely the advanced methods that we later present. You'll be more than familiar with the basic mushroom life cycle after you've performed this method once or twice, and ready to move on.

### The "Improved" PF Tek

Materials 40 mL (meager '/4 cup) natural brown rice flour (per jar)

140 mL ('/2 cup) vermiculite (per jar), in addition to extra for casing layer

Water 1/2-16 ounces (250 mL) mason jars Aluminum foil Spore-water syringe(s)

### Alcohol lamp or butane lighter Rubbing alcohol

Material Notes: Brown rice flour is accessible at some health food stores, or you can pound your own in a little coffee processor or zest factory. The jars ought to be straight sided Gelly jars), without the shoulders present on larger-sized canning jars. Faucet water is fine; however, you can use bottled or refined if your water source is suspect.

Sterilization Note: This method contains the one occurrence right now we depict a boiling water shower cleansing of a substrate as a choice to pressure-cooking. The water shower process is effective, yet not 1 00% reliable; some percentage of jars prepared with it will at present be likely to taint. In the event that you have a pressure cooker, you should use it here as well; if not, presently is as good a time as any to get one.

1. Depending on the number of jars you will vaccinate (a 10 mL syringe contains enough answer for immunize 8-10 jars), place the necessary measure of vermiculite in a bowl. Presently evacuate around 5% of this and place it in a separate container.

2. Into the principle bowl of vermiculite, add water a little at a time, mixing as you go, until the mixture can't hold any longer and tl1ere is only a slight overabundance of water at the bottom of the bowl. Presently add the held dry material and mix completely. The vermiculite should now be at "field capacity," implying that it contains the most extreme measure of water it can easily hold.

3. Empty the brown rice flour into the bowl and mix well, covering the vermiculite grains with a layer of moistened flour.

4. Spoon this mixture into the jars, leaving a level 1/2-inch (1-centimeter) hole at the top. Place it into the jars freely and don't pack it down; keeping an open, breezy structure will permit the mycelium to breath and grow at an ideal rate. Take a clammy paper towel and wipe down the sides and around within edges of the jars to completely expel any wanderer substrate, which could somehow turn into a source of contamination.

5. Occupy the rest of the space of the jar with dry vermiculite. This layer will at first go about as a hindrance to contaminants, which, should they by one way or another find their way

inside the jar, would be prevented from coming into contact with the substrate. Afterward, it will fill in as the casing soil, from which the mushrooms will fruit.

6.  Take two 5-inch square bits of aluminum foil and wrap them firmly over the mouth of the jar. Freely screw lids onto the jars, taking care not to tear the foil beneath. (The use of lids in the PF Tek is discretionary yet provides an additional layer of assurance.)

7.  Burden the jars into your pressure cooker, along with the proper measure of water, and sanitize the jars at 15 psi for 45 minutes. If there is sufficient room, the jars might be stacked in more than one layer.

Or then again (Boiling Water Bath Method):

8.  Place the jars in a large cooking pot in a solitary layer, along with enough water to bring it to about halfway up the sides of the jars. Spread the pot and boil for 1 .5 hours. Check once in a while to make sure the water level stays steady, adding water as vital.

## Phase 2: PF Tek Inoculation

1.  When the jars have cooled down to room temperature, put them on a clean working surface, together with the spore-water syringe and alcohol lamp. Replace the lids and drop the cover over the top foil.

2.  Remove the cover from the syringe, rub the needle with a moistened alcohol, clean paper towel or cotton ball, and place the tip of the

needle in your lamp's flame until it begins glowing red (be careful to keep the plastic end of the needle away from the flame, and be careful when using alcohol near an open flame).

3. Using one container at a time, removing the top layer of tape, shaking the syringe gently to disperse the spore solution, and injecting a small amount into the jar at four equally spaced dots right inside the inner rim. Insert 1 inch (2 cm) of needle into the jar so its point passes the dry layer of vermiculite, then squeeze out a few drops. You should be in a spot to see the solution run down the jar sides. Repeat on three points left. Every jar should get 1-1, 5 mL total solution.

4. Inject all the jars in the same way, covering the top layer of foil and cap (if used) at each. Label the outside of the jars with relevant information and/or notebook number, and position in a clean, warm spot to incubate.

**Phase 3: Incubation**

The jars should be incubated in the 75-850 F range, at a warm, draft-free location. If your home temperature is consistently within this range, then it should be sufficient to simply store them in a clean box. If not, an incubator box will ensure healthy and rapid growth, and is easy to build from a cooler and a few items that you can buy from a pet store's reptile department.

## Materials

- ✓ 25–50 gallon plastic or Styrofoam cooler
- ✓ 8-watt reptile heating mat
- ✓ Flexible indoor regulator controller
- ✓ Air temperature thermometer

Place the heating mat and thermometer in the cooler, plug the mat in and switch on the temperature controller. Set the controller to its lowest setting and let the cooler warm up for a few hours before switching it up step by step until it reaches a steady 80 ° or something like this. Arrange the heating mat on one side of the cooler, and stack your jars on the contrary side, as a long way from direct heat as could be allowed. Depending on the surrounding temperature of the room, you may need to incidentally alter the indoor regulator to keep a consistent temperature inside the cooler. At the point when surrounding temperatures go above 85°, you'll have to make sense of a way to shield the jars from overheating. Right now, then developing an elaborate refrigeration gadget, your most logical option is to store them in a shut container in a cool spot in your home, for example, an unheated basement. If no such place is accessible to you, this would be a good time to take a break for some time, until outside temperatures have cooled adequately to continue cultivation.

### Phase 4: Germination/Colonization

Within a week or so, the first signs of spore germination in your jars will start to appear. Look for tiny pinpoints of bright white fozzy growth, usually directly below the injection points near the base of the jar. Those tiny colonies radiate outward in time to form individual mycelium spheres. The spheres inside each jar will join each other within 10 days to a few weeks, and the jar will be fully colonized.

### Contamination

The jar is likely to be contaminated if you see any growth in your jars that is not pure white in color and should be removed from the incubator immediately and disposed of. Molds which tend to have highly colored spores in shades of blue, green, black or pink will be the most common offenders. On the other hand, bacterial contamination will appear as spots of wet, sticky blobs on the jar's inner surface, and may be accompanied by a sour or rotten smell of apples. Remember to always remove contaminated culture containers from your work and growing areas, and thoroughly clean the containers before returning them to your workspace.

### Phase 5: Fruiting

Once the jars have colonized completely, they're ready to be fruited. At this stage, the lids and foil are removed, the top layer of vermiculite is moistened, and the jars are put under a light source, either by artificial light given by a dedicated fluorescent "grow" light or by a brightly lit window. Since P cubensis requires light to stimulate fruiting, and you want to limit fruiting to the upper surface of the cakes, you need to restrict light exposure to just that area of the jars in some way. This can be done in numerous numbers of ways, such as wrapping the jars in aluminum foil, or thick, opaque paper strips. One simple method that we used is to place the jars inside short pieces of cardboard tubing, such as the type used to store posters, cut to come just above the rim.

### Preparing the Jars for Fruiting

1. Remove the lids and foil from each jar. You may see a few "fans" of mycelium jabbing up through the vermiculite layer.

2. Wipe a spotless fork with some alcohol, permit it to evaporate, and afterward delicately scratch (not scratch off) the dry vermiculite layer right down to the top of the cake underneath, to break up and equitably circulate the mycelial parts within.

3. Take a spray mister of clean water and mist the vermiculite until it is saturated (it will darken slightly in color; when you can see free streaming water, that is enough.)

4. Repeat with each jar, cleaning the fork each time to prevent inadvertently spreading contaminants.

5. At the point when the entirety of the jars is ready, place them in singular cardboard cylinders inside an encased container, for example, a large clear plastic bag (cut or perforate it to give a few gas exchange) or a reasonable plastic stockpiling tub.

6. If you are utilizing a fluorescent grow light, set your timer to an 8-hour on 1 16-hour off cycle; in any case, simply find the jars in a sufficiently bright area, for example, close to a radiant window. The ideal temperature of your

growing area ought to be in the 65-75°F range, slightly lower than that required during colonization.

7. Mist the casing lightly a few times every day to replace any water lost to vanishing.

You should see primordia begin to form within a couple of days to about fourteen days. They will no doubt grow inside the casing layer and will not be visible until small-scale mushrooms are already established all around. They tend to grow astonishingly quickly when they have accomplished this scale and may seem to arrive at full size virtually medium term. They will draw water from the cake and the casing layer as they expand, so make sure to increase misting varying to keep the vermiculite saturated, always taking care not to overwater.

**Phase 6:** Harvesting when the mushroom has reached a suitable size for successful spore dispersal, it stops growing and increases its cap to expose the atmosphere to its spore-providing gills. This argument is only followed by the best time to pick your mushrooms, as a single mushroom can release a galactic amount of spores, which can make things incredibly chaotic. When the mushroom prepares to reveal its gills the best way to tell is to pay close consideration to the partial veil, the thin protective film that covers them. At first, when the cap is completely inserted (looking a lot like those good old streetlamps globe-on - a-shaft), the partial veil is covered up). As the cap starts to grow, the veil forms around the cap's bottom hemisphere as a round, light-colored band.

When the cap begins to flatten out, the partial veil gets extended past its ability to expand and begins to tear, pulling away from the external edges of the gills. Eventually, the partial veil withdraws from the cap altogether, and its remainders stay joined to the stipe in a skirt-like ring, known as an annulus). Ideally, you need to pick your mushrooms when the partial veil is visible, or at the most recent, before it begins to break. Harvesting the mushrooms is as basic as getting a handle on them at the base and winding tenderly while pulling them far up into the clouds from the casing. In the event that your fingers are small and deft enough, you can use your spotless hands to do as such; if not, a pair of clean chopsticks makes a good harvesting apparatus. Any piece of the mushroom that remaining parts behind in the casing will rot, so take care to remove everything, down to the base of the stipe. Do whatever it takes not to touch the casing layer and take uncommon care not to harm close by less-created mushrooms or primordia. Sometimes, be that as it may, it is difficult to avoid upsetting or evacuating close by mushrooms while expelling another. Right now, is smarter to remove these "babies" also, as opposed to leaving them behind. Often, upsetting them cuts off their association with the substrate and they stop growing and eventually rot. What vitality the culture would somehow, or another have expended on these fruits will be occupied to other people, so don't stress a lot over the infrequent loss.

Normally, a decent measure of vermiculite will be adhered to the base of the harvested mushrooms, leaving behind a divot in the casing layer. When you are done harvesting, simply fill these holes with fresh vermiculite, mist the casing altogether and return the jars to their fruiting area. During the period immediately following a harvest, increment misting recurrence altogether, so as to replace the substantial measure of dampness removed from the cakes.

Each jar should produce three to five yields, or flushes, of mushrooms, with about seven days of recovery time between each harvest. During the later flushes, when the supplements of the substrate are substantially drained, the cakes will shrink and pull away from the sides of the jar, uncovering the dividers of the cakes to the atmosphere and to light. Mushrooms will at that point begin to form around the sides of the cakes. Aside fro111. Being increasingly difficult to remove totally from the jar, these are not an issue (this is the place a pair of chopsticks proves to be useful).

After the fourth or fifth flush, the jars will be almost completely drained, and the number of mushrooms that form will be insignificant. Now, the cakes ought to be discarded, since the mycelium in them will begin to pass on and will eventually rot, turning into a vector for contamination.

# CHAPTER 5

## *Working with agar*

**P**reparing Agar Plates

Mushroom crops are usually grown out on nitrified agar plates and maintained. The agar's smooth, semi-solid surface provides an outspread, two-dimensional growth pattern, taking into account the easy evaluation of a crop and the distinctive proof of and separation from any pollutants that should arise. Agar is a polysaccharide (a sugar-like atom) found in the cell dividers of certain green growth. At the point when disintegrated in boiling water and afterward cooled, agar partially solidifies, much like gelatin.

Agar itself gives no sustenance to the fungus, so a variety of supplements are added to the medium, for example, malt sugar and yeast extract. The fixings are combined with water in a heatproof container, sterilized in a pressure cooker, and filled Petri dishes while still fluid. One of the media most commonly used is Malt-Yeast Extract Agar, or MYA, for short. It is a generally useful medium, one on which all species of Psilocybe will grow gracefully.

## Senescence

Growers often interchange media recipes to avoid strain senescence, the corruption of a culture because of maturing. Sometimes after a number of transfers between plates, a culture can begin to grow feebly, or even stop growing inside and out. Senescent cultures tend to fruit inadequately or not in the slightest degree and are typically discarded for re-separation of a healthy strain from spores.

The causes of strain senescence are yet not surely knowing; however, it appears to occur frequently when a culture is maintained on similar media recipe for a long timeframe. Fungi (like humans) appear to do best when given a variety of foods to expend, and like us they grow exhausted and even pass on when given something very similar to eat day in, day out. To avoid senescence, it is basic that you change your media recipe each time you use it, which "works out" the fungus, provoking it to produce various sets of proteins constantly. One basic way to do this is to add small quantities of grain flour to each bunch, rotating the type you use each time you pour new plates, as portrayed underneath. Once in a while, in any case, you should challenge your fungus considerably further, by requesting that it grow on a completely novel medium. This can be especially useful for restoring a culture that begins to show evidence of debilitating. Right now, need to reject every basic sugar and starches completely, and give it something completely novel to process. (We call this recipe "Anything" Agar.)

It might grow gradually on the new medium, however following half a month of growth, when you move it back to an increasingly balanced medium like MYA, it is likely to detonate with new growth. What would it be a good idea for you to feed it? Any cellulose, starch, or sugar will do, including soybeans, paper pellets, raspberry jam, nutty spread whatever you can think of. The sky's the point of confinement. We have even known about one cultivator who took care of his fungi dried crickets he found at a pet store! Now and again you may find a material that your fungi refuse to grow on. Assuming this is the case, no issue, simply take a stab at something else. Another way to avoid strain debasement is to limit the number of transfers of each culture that you perform.

- ✓ Malt Yeast Agar [MYA) Medium
- ✓ 22 g agar
- ✓ 12 g light malt extract
- ✓ 1 g yeast extract
- ✓ 1/4 tsp natural grain flour (rotate among oats, cornmeal, amaranth, rice, millet, rye or some other starch or sugar you can think of)
- ✓ 5 g wood fuel pellets or hardwood sawdust
- ✓ 1 L faucet water 8 mL 3% hydrogen peroxide (discretionary, added after sanitization and cooling; see underneath.)

1. Add every single dry fixing to jar, followed by the water. Make certain to use a jar that is 1 .5 to 2 times the volume of media wanted, so it

doesn't boil over during cleansing. Attachment the neck of the bottle with cotton fleece, at that point wrap the opening and neck of the bottle with aluminum foil.

2. Put the jar in the pressure cooker along with the necessary measure of water. If you will add peroxide to the agar, make certain to sterilize a few estimating pipettes too, wrapped in aluminum toil to keep up sterility before use.

3. Sterilize at 15 psi for 30 min. Try not to cook your agar media for longer than 45 minutes, since this can cause the media to caramelize, and fungi don't grow well on caramelized sugars.

4. Permit the pressure cooker to come to atmospheric pressure, at that point carefully move the jar and pipettes to a glove enclose or front of a stream hood while still hot. It is helpful to use a few layers of clean paper towel as a potholder while moving items from the pressure cooker to the workspace.

5. When using peroxide: apply 8 mL of 3 percent hydrogen peroxide, using a sterile channel e or calculating spoon, until the outside of the container is co ('} l enough to handle quickly yet very warm at the same time (between 1' 0 °-140 ° F). In the two headings, rotate the medium gently a few times to blend it in altogether. Be careful not to over-agitate it and build bubbles that end up in your dishes.

6. Open your Petri dishes sleeves as planned on the bundling and stack them directly onto your work area. To later power carry plastic jacket.

7. Operating with stacks of ten plates one after the other, raise the entire stack by the lid of the bottom plate in one hand, leaving the bottom half on the top of the table, and slowly dump just enough medium into the plate to completely cover it. Replace the stack, and repeat until complete, with the plate above. One liter of average will suffice for regular Petri dishes of 20-30 1 00 mm. Make an effort not to agitate when you pour in the mixture. When solid particles are at the bottom of the cup, leave them there; all usable nutrients should be in arrangement, and you need the media on your plates to be transparent enough to see through.

8. If you find that the agar starts to solidify before you finish pouring it, holding the jar in a shallow pot of hot (1 50 ° F) water when not being used is often beneficial.

9. Stack the finished plates in a single section, and freely replace the sleeve they came in to permit each plate in the stack to cool gradually and uniformly, limiting buildup on the upper plates (buildup can make the agar difficult to see, and can turn into a vector for contamination). A similar effect can be accomplished by covering each stack with a spotless coffee cup or substantial glass half-loaded up with hot water.

10. Permit plates to cool medium-term.

11. Peroxide plates can be left for a few days in a cool sans draft spot to additionally drive off any residual buildup. Lay them out in stacks of a few, inexactly secured with a couple of sheets of clean waxed paper. Plates without peroxide ought to be placed in sleeves when they have cooled.

12. Slide the plastic sleeve back over the plates and tape it shut firmly with clear pressing tape. Store them agar side up (to additionally limit buildup) in a cool and dry place until required.

### Care of Petri Dishes and Cultures

When making transfers, lids ought to be removed for as brief a time as could be expected under the circumstances, and held legitimately over the plate to keep contaminants out.

Cultures ought to be stockpiled side up too. Be that as it may, it is a good plan to give new transfers a day or so to grow out onto the new plate before flipping around them, or the moved material probably won't hold fast to the fresh agar surface. Culture plates ought to be wrapped around their edges with a few layers of parafilm.

### Spore Streaking

Even if you use PF Tek to grow P. cubensis mushrooms or collect fresh specimens from the wild, you will need to start your crops from spores to isolate a strain of pure fruiting. There are two methods you can use to start cultivation of mushrooms from spores to agar. A sterile inoculating loop is used in the conventional system to extract a small measure of the spores from a print, and then streaked over an agar plate. Remember that you cannot use Petri plates containing peroxide for this reason, as it would slaughter the spores. On the other side, spores are sprouted in clean cardboard circles in an innovative process developed by Rush Wayne and illustrated in volume two of his book Growing Mushrooms the Easy Way.

This method gives a few unmistakable advantages over the traditional method. The small size of the circles and the tight openings of the test tubes help keep contaminants out of cultures that are unprotected by peroxide. In addition, it is a genuinely fast system: the circles are immediately colonized and would then be able to be placed legitimately onto peroxidated agar.

Finally, because the circle demonstrations both as the substrate and as the instrument used to lift spores from the spore print, it accommodates a proficient exchange, which is particularly helpful when the spore print is black out and light on spores. Utilizing a punching tool, small circles are cut from thin, flat cardboard (the gray sheets found at the back of stack of paper are great). These are moistened slightly, placed in a jar and sterilized along with test tubes containing 5-10 drops of a malt-yeast extract solution. At the point when cool, the circles are used to pick up a small amount of spores, and afterward dropped into the tube, where they ingest the malt solution. In time, the spores develop and when the modest circles are fully colonized, they are transferred to peroxide agar plates.

### Agar Spore Germination

This method is indistinguishable from the one used when making spore-water syringes, apart from that here the spores are transferred to sans peroxide agar plates instead of water.

### Materials

- ✓ Spore print
- ✓ Sans peroxide agar
- ✓ Petri dishes
- ✓ Inoculating loop
- ✓ Alcohol lamp

### Parafilm

1. Heat the inoculation loop inside the alcohol lamp in your glove box or flow hood until it sparks out super-hot.

2. Using your other hand to lift the lid of the first Petri dish, touch the tip of the loop to the focal point of the agar to cool it (this also places a thin agar film on the loop, which will allow the spores to stick to it).

3. Cover the plate and afterward use the loop to pick up a small number of spores from your print.

4. Streak these across the Petri dish in a S-shaped movement and afterward close the plate.

5. Re-sterilize and cool the loop before marking each plate.

6. Wrap the edges of every plate with parafilm after inoculation, mark them with any applicable information, and hatch agar side up.

## Cardboard Disk Spore Germination

## Materials

- ✓ Spore print
- ✓ Cardboard circles
- ✓ J/2-pint jar and lid Screw-capped test tubes or vials (2 or 3 for each spore print)
- ✓ Malt-yeast agar solution (1 tsp malt and a little pinch of yeast extract in 1 00 mL water)
- ✓ Pipette or eyedropper
- ✓ Tweezers
- ✓ Alcohol lamp

## Parafilm

1. Place cardboard circles in J/2-pint jar, along with 1 - 2m1 water, and seal. Place 5-10 drops of malt solution into test tubes and lightly seal. Sterilize the jar and tubes for 15 minutes at 45 psi and permit to cool completely.

2. Place your glove box or flow hood with all the tools and materials.

3. Heat the alcohol lamp tweezers up to high and allow to cool.

4. Open the jar and extract one circle using tweezers. Spread jar.

5. Lightly touch the edge of the circle to part of the spore print. You ought to have the option to see the black spores holding fast to the plate.

6. Open a test tube and drop the plate onto the bottom of the tube.

7. Repeat 3-5 times for every tube.

8. Create in any event two tubes of plates for every spore print.

9. Seal the tubes with parafilm and hatch.

10. At the point when the spores have sprouted and the circles are fully colonized, move a couple to singular peroxide-containing agar plates.

### Incubation

Vaccinated culture plates and spore circles ought to be hatched in a warm, sans draft area, in the 75-85° F range. In the event that the temperature in your home is consistently within this range, at that point it is adequate to simply store them in a perfect box.

### Tissue Transfers (Cloning)

Clean, fresh, mushrooms, either fruited from a multispore culture (from a PF Tek jar, for instance), or gathered from the wild, can likewise be used to start an agar culture. Right now, coming about culture ought to be a solitary strain and should display indistinguishable attributes from its parent.

Since it is hereditarily indistinguishable from the strain from which it was secluded, it is viewed as a clone, and this procedure is known as cloning. Because of this, we generally search for the healthiest specimens in a populace to clone, with the hope of isolating a strain that will furnish consistent and dynamic fruitings with each use. Good characters to search for in a parent incorporate early, large, or thick fruits, and any that have a healthy look in general. Isolating a solitary, fruiting strain is as basic as picking the choicest specimens from your yields and culturing them on agar.

The mushrooms are torn or cut open in a glove box or flow hood, and a small piece of clean mycelium is removed from the inside of the stipe or the area of the cap simply over the gills and placed on a fresh agar plate. After a short brooding period, the mycelial fragments grow out onto the plate and would then be able to be subcultured. Often nonetheless, for unknown reasons, clones taken from a similar parent mushroom do display varying mycelial qualities.

Consequently, we make various (at least four) cultures from everyone, and spare simply the best coming about cultures for additional use. Looks can be beguiling and strains may not perform as predicted by their appearance, so we clone the same number of various specimens as time and space permits, so as to enhance our chances of achievement over the long haul. Because they have never been exposed to the outer condition, the cells on the inside of a mushroom ought to be clean (i.e., uncontaminated). To ensure sterility, be that as it may, you ought to always attempt to clone mushrooms at the earliest opportunity in the wake of picking them. If you can't use them immediately, you can store them in the ice chest in a clean Tupperware container fixed with a fresh paper towel for a couple of days, yet very little longer. Unlike while streaking spores, peroxide in the agar media will really enhance your chances of effective cloning, since it gives an additional layer of protection from contaminants. Accordingly, we strongly recommend utilizing peroxidated agar at whatever point doing tissue cultures, except if you find that the species or strain being referred to doesn't tolerate it.

**Tissue Transfers**

**Materials Mushroom(s)**

✓ Petri dishes (with peroxide)

✓ Scalpel

✓ Alcohol

✓ Alcohol lamp

✓ Cotton balls or paper towel

1. Before use, mushrooms for cloning should be cleaned entirely of any free casing material. If possible 2 this job should be finished away from the workplace. Preferably dealing with an alcohol-soaked cotton ball in your glove box or flow hood cleans the mushroom's outer surfaces.

2. Sterilize the alcohol lamp with scalpel. Press the mushroom delicately between your thumb and index finger, holding it at the base of the

stipe. You should have the option to divide it along the centerline, and then strip the mushroom's two halves divided the long way, if possible, entirely through the cap. If it is a small example, or is not parting effectively, you can use the scalpel instead to open it. Try to avoid allowing the blade to legally touch the region from which you need to clone, as it may pose pollutants in your culture on the outer surfaces of the mushroom.

3.  After each use, sterilize the cutting edge again.

4.  Cut a small piece of mycelium from a reasonable area of the stipe or cap (generally at the thickest, most thickly packed area) with your Petri dishes ready. It should be as big a chunk as might be expected under the circumstances, preferably from 3-8 mm wide and long. Be particularly careful not to cut right through to the mushroom's unsterile outer layers.

5.  Lance the mycelium fragment gently onto your scalpel end. Lift the Petri dish lid in your other hand, place the fragment in the center of the agar and close the plate afterwards. (Sometimes the stringy idea of the mycelium will cause it to stick to the tip of the sharp edge of the scalpel; assuming this is the case, take a slice to cut through the fragment and push it down into the agar as you are doing as such.)

6.  Repeat with at least three plates for each mushroom.

7. Seal the plates with parafilm, mark them properly, and place them in your hatchery. Store them straight up until they begin to grow out, and afterward turn around them not surprisingly. You should begin to see growth within a couple of days to seven days. From the start, the fragment will turn out to be uniformly fluffy, as its cells begin to isolate once more; eventually the mycelium will fan out from where it contacts the agar to colonize the whole plate.

## Agar-to-Agar Transfers (Sub culturing)

A small piece of healthy-looking mycelium from the edge of a crop is cut out with a sterile scalpel and placed on the center of another plate to make agar-to-agar transfers. Growing cultures should be used or subcultured before the mycelium gets too close to the edge of the plate, since the outer edges of the plate will harbor pollutants, which would be protected under the progressive mycelial front, only to grow when they are moved to another media.

Any part of the propelling edge could be subcultured in the event the society is a mere strain. If it's a multi-strain culture (for example, that emerging from multispore inoculation), then you'll need to select mycelium with the ideal attributes at that point. The presence of at least two forms of mycelia within a solitary community is called sectoring. The visual appearance of a stable strain varies equally from species to species, but thick rhizomorphic development for all Psilocybe species is a good sign of general health. Consider divisions with moderate growth or wispy-looking mycelium which are less likely to produce a strain of fruiting.

Also put the agar wedge face down on the fresh plate, while making a move. That serves two major capacities. Above all, it brings the mycelium in direct contact with the agar, advancing the new plate's rapid colonization. Furthermore, by sandwiching the mycelium between two layers of agar containing peroxide, any contaminant spores or micro-organisms that store away on the mycelial surface are destroyed.

### Agar-to-Agar Transfers

### Materials

- ✓ Agar culture (s)
- ✓ Sterile agar plates
- ✓ Scalpel Alcohol lamp

### Parafilm

1. In a glove box or flow hood, remove any parafilm from the outside of your healthy culture dish.

2. Heat the edge of the scalpel in your alcohol lamp until it gleams, at that point cool it in a fresh Petri dish.

3. Holding the lid of the first culture dish slightly, cut squares or wedges of agar and mycelium from the ideal segments of the plate, from 1/2 to 1 centimeter wide. For the good of simplicity, you may cut more than each wedge in turn.

4.  To make the transfer, you have to remove the lid of the first culture plate completely. With the blade in one hand, lift the lid of the perfect plate slightly to the other side, skewer one wedge of agar from the culture plate on the tip of the blade and place it on the center of the new plate, mycelium side down.

5.  Repeat on all plates, seal and imprint suitably, and place in the hatchery, upside down not surprisingly. (Wedges of agar stick well to fresh agar, permitting the plates to be altered immediately.)

## Contamination

Contamination in cultivation of mushrooms is inescapable. One of the benefits of operating with the two-dimensional agar plate surface is that pollutants are readily detected and isolated from balanced cultures. Plates which offer some indication of contamination should be removed from the growing area and immediately discarded.

Every so often, it might be important to attempt to "salvage" a debased culture (in the event that you always do multiple indistinguishable transfers and keep clean work propensities, such events ought to be incredibly uncommon.) In this case, you ought to always move the culture away from its contaminants to another plate. In the event that you attempt to remove contaminants from an agar dish by cutting the intruders from the plate, you will likely just spread the contamination further. Because form spores are so handily upset, it is exceedingly difficult to avoid moving contaminants along with your culture to new plates and may take a few transfers before they are fully disposed of.

### Diagnosing the Sources of Contamination on Agar

You can often determine the source of contaminants on agar by observing the example of the contamination on the plate.

1. If contamination shows up before the plates are used, it very well may be a sign of lacking disinfection of the agar, poor sterile strategy during pouring or capacity of the plates, or an inadequate convergence of peroxide in the medium.

2. If signs of contamination occur on the outrageous edges of the plate, either in singular settlements or in a total ring, it can show that non-sterile air had been drawn into the plates as they cooled. To prevent this, let the agar cool adequately before pouring it, and spread the plates with their plastic sleeve immediately in the wake of filling them.

3. Contamination beginning at the inoculation point means that either a debased parent culture or deficient cleansing of the blade or inoculation loop. Look at cultures to be transferred carefully before utilizing them and avoid utilizing any that are suspect. Always heat inoculating tools until they spark scorching.

4. Bacterial contamination shows up as disgusting, gleaming, translucent roundabout provinces, often white, pink, or yellow in color.

Microbes thrive in wet situations and are effortlessly spread onto plates with overabundance buildup on their lids. Always hold up until agar has cooled adequately before pouring, let plates cool gradually in their plastic sleeve, and store them agar side up.

### Long-Term Strain Storage

When you have disengaged a healthy fruiting strain, you will need some way to spread this equivalent strain for a long time, with the goal that you don't need to continually repeat the detachment procedure. Cloning from plate to plate again and again will eventually cause the strain to senesce, regardless of whether you modify your agar recipe consistently, as we recommend. Along these lines, you always need to use cultures that have been exposed to as barely any transfers as could be expected under the circumstances. To do this, you ought to create an "ace" culture of any strain you think about deserving of proliferation, as soon you distinguish it. The ace culture is then placed into refrigerated, long-term stockpiling, and subcultured varying. Cultures that are stored at standard fridge temperatures (38° F) enter a condition of suspended animation and can be restored by simply sub culturing them to a fresh plate. After a short recovery period, the culture will continue ordinary growth. We recommend putting away cultures on sterilized paper pellets in test tubes. Strains stored on agar can cease to exist out of the blue, maybe inferable from the high sugar content of the media. The wholesome content of paper is insignificant, yet apparently adequate to keep the culture healthy for long periods.

The limited mouths of test tubes are ideal for ' limiting buildup and contamination, and their small size takes into consideration easy capacity. However, in the event that you don't approach test tubes, you can use 1/2-pint mason jars or other similar small autoclavable containers. In the wake of transferring the culture to the tube and permitting it to grow out, the tubes are placed in an auxiliary container, (for example, a Ziploc bag) and stored in the refrigerator. Strains kept along these lines can stay practical for a long time, yet it is a good plan to recover cultures intermittently (when consistently or two) by sub culturing each to a plate, at that point coming back to fresh paper for additional capacity. The effects of peroxide on cultures stored for long periods are not notable and subsequently we keep it separate from our capacity media.

### Paper Pellet Storage Medium

### Materials

✓ Paper pellet feline litter

✓ Faucet water Test tubes or other reasonable containers

### A channel

1. Moisten paper pellets to field capacity.

2. Burden inside pipe, absolute' 10' /2. Be vigilant to avoid any medium bits from the outside of the tubing. Seal for free.

3. Put the containers in your pressure cooker and sterilize in layers for 30 minutes at 15 psi. Jars,

while test tubes should be put in a rack or a wire to hold them upright.

4. At the point when the cooker has come back to atmospheric pressure yet is still warm to the touch, open it, and carefully transfer the containers to your glove box and permit to cool.

## Inoculating Storage Tubes

Paper pellet tubes are vaccinated similarly to Petri dishes. Because the cultures lack peroxide, and they are intended to be stored as long as possible, you should take additional care to avoid presenting contaminants while doing as such, following all the standard precautions. In addition, you ought to sterilize the neck of the inclination tube each time it is opened, by moving it in the fire of your alcohol lamp.

1. Fire the scalpel and the neck of the open tube.

2. Cut a small piece of agar out of a healthy culture and put it in the tube of the sawdust. Since the test tube necks are too limited to even consider allowing the blade to penetrate, it is easier to hold the tube on a level plane, place the wedge on the upper mass of the tube, seal it, and then thump it onto the sawdust delicately afterward.

3. Seal the jar, cover the cap or lid with a parafilm band and print it out properly.

4. Hatch until the paper is fully colonized, at that point place the tubes into an optional

container, for example, a cooler bag or Tupperware container and refrigerate.

## Recovering Cultures from Storage

To recover a culture from its stockpiling container, return the culture to room temperature for 48 hours, and transfer (under the standard clean conditions) a small chunk of mycelium-secured paper from the capacity container to a fresh, peroxidated agar Petri dish.

# CHAPTER 6

## *Fruiting containers*

When you have a completely colonized substratum, it must be put in a suitable container for casing and fruiting. The container you choose depends on the quantity of substrate to be fruited and can range from a small aluminum foil bread dish to a large receptacle for plastic transport. You will concentrate on 2-3 inches of substratum depth when fruiting smaller quantities of grain, and as much as 6 inches for larger quantities. Besides scale, while picking a fruiting container, there are sure features to consider. It should be made of a material that is sufficiently unbending to keep the substratum in place as it colonizes, and it should be completely opaque, allowing you to absorb light alone on the surface of the casing soil. Furthermore, the container's absolute depth should preferably be close to doubling the substratum depth to allow simple exchange of gas when opening the container for misting.

For example, a few growers use smaller, fully enclosed containers, plastic canisters with Snap-On spreads to create a moist environment. While this does work, it requires cutting or drilling holes in the container sides to allow exchange of gas, and it ensures that the top must be transparent at any rate to allow light to fall on the surface of the shell. Alternatively, we recommend using shallower, opaque containers which are then put inside the clammy, a fruiting chamber's sufficiently bright setting.

The fruiting chamber can be as straightforward as an unmistakable plastic bag perforated to allow exchange of gas, positioned nearly a sunlit window, or as complex as a multi-layered shelf device that holds multiple containers, fitted with synchronized blinding lights and a humidification.

The two types of fruiting containers that we often use are plastic dishwasher tubes, 1 1.5"x 13.5"x 5 "wide, which hold 4-8 quarter jars or one bag of grain, or 20"x Is'' X 7 "deep plastic containers for larger quantities of substrates. The smaller dishpans are sold in equipment and kitchen supply stores, and the conveyor receptacles can mostly be bought at the café supply battle.

### The Humidity Tent

The cased containers must be kept in a humid environment to prevent fast loss of dampness from the casing and substrate. Unlike numerous other cultivated mushrooms that require significant levels of relative humidity (90%-100%), we have found that Psilocybe cubensis does fine and dandy with much lower levels (down to 70%).As long as the container is placed in a nook that is adequately small, and the casing soil is kept very much watered, enough water will wick into the immediate environment to keep the mushrooms glad.. Smaller plate or tubs can simply be placed into clear plastic bags and tied shut.

Holes ought to be punched or cut in the top and sides of the bag to take into consideration gas exchange, with four or five 1/2-inch holes per square foot. (A few online mushroom providers sell pre-perforated bags precisely for this purpose.) The container ought to be removed from the bag during misting to help displace amassed carbon dioxide. The bags ought to be sufficiently large to oblige the growing mushrooms, which will extend as much as 8 inches over the top of the casing soil.

Larger single containers can be placed inside rearranged clear plastic storage tubes, with holes bored for gas exchange in their sides, or placed on a tented shelf frame. A variety of garden supply catalogs and online retailers sell "rising racks". These are three or four-layered lightweight racks enclosed inside a zippered plastic tent for moisture control. At the point when these make excellent individual mushroom growing fenced in areas when combined with a controlled lighting system. Can shelf can hold a few smaller containers or one transportation tank, with plenty of space to house the creating mushrooms in between each shelf.

## Humidity Levels

Small fruiting containers ought to go into perforated plastic bags, single larger ones ought to go into large bags or clear tubs, and multiple larger ones can be placed on an encased grow rack. For whatever length of time that the size of the humidity chamber is firmly matched to the amount of substrate it contains, the dampness levels within ought to be genuinely easy to keep up with a more than once per day hand misting.

At the point when the casing soil is all around watered, it should wick enough water into the immediate environment to keep the growing mushrooms cheerful. In the event that the air in your growing area happens to be especially dry, you may need to fall back on a beneficial humidification system. Right now, least for the small-to-medium scale grower, the best scale is a cool mist (Impeller) style humidifier, which doesn't use heat to create humidity and, in this way, won't superfluously raise the temperatures of your trimming area. These are modest and readily accessible at most larger pharmacies and retail chains.

We have seen different growers develop entangled tubing systems for siphoning soggy air from a humidifier into a grow rack. This might be essential while fruiting large numbers of containers one after another, however in general the humidifier itself can simply be placed on one of the racks alongside the plate. Buildup will develop on the dividers of the enclosure, so it is a good plan to place a large plate beneath the rack to shield dampness from falling legitimately onto the floor. Unfilled and clean this plate often to avoid form development.

## Lighting

Your lighting setup ought to likewise be scaled suitably to your fruiting area. Psilocybe mushrooms are unlike plants in their lighting requirements. They use light just to animate growth, not as a vitality source, and they just require short day by day times of it to fruit successfully. A good general guideline is that if the space is lit adequately to see well, it should support fruiting fine and dandy. A couple PF Jars or a solitary tub will require minimal in excess of a south-bound window or good encompassing electrical lighting. Larger grow racks will require an inherent lighting setup. We have found that 15-20-watt conservative bright light bulbs work dependably well and use almost no vitality.

However, they ought to be mounted outside the grow chamber (maybe mounted to a contiguous divider) to limit heating and reduce the risk of an electrical short out. Depending on the size and number of containers in the enclosure, it might be important to mount lamps at a few areas so as to avoid throwing shadows on the cultures. Electric lighting systems ought to likewise be put on timers, set to enlighten the space for 8 hours out of every day.

# CHAPTER 7

## *Casing soil*

**M**ost cultivated species of mushrooms, like Psilocybe cubensis, can yield rich fruit only if the substratum is covered in a soil-like layer known as a casing layer. For example, peat moss or vermiculite, along with gypsum and calcium carbonate, are typically composed of non-nutritious materials with high water-holding capacities. The casing layer serves a number of important mushrooms producing capacities. The coating is helping to protect the substratum from losing its moisture to the atmosphere because of its high-water content. It provides a humid microenvironment within which the delicate primordia can develop, and it serves as a water-saving to draw on the parched mushrooms as they grow. Since the case layer takes up and discharges water like a wash, it also helps a grower to hold a bed comfortably at its ideal level of moisture thus reducing the risk of waterlogging the substratum and suffocating the fungus.

Furthermore, the amount of moisture on the particulate casing layer is often easier to "catch" than on exposed colonized soil, thereby enhancing the humidification process. Many recipes for the casing soil include mineral salts, such as chalk and gypsum. To some degree, peat moss is acidic, and mushroom mycelium often oozes acidic metabolites as they grow. Since a highly acidic atmosphere can damage the fungus and support the growth of microscopic organisms, the addition of chalk (calcium carbonate) to the casing soil helps to maintain a slightly necessary condition (a pH of 7.5-8.5). Gypsum (calcium sulfate) is added to help preserve a free, vaporous structure, and provide the developing fungus with mineral sustenance as calcium and sulfur. Assumed "water crystals" are arbitrary fixations that you can apply to your casing mix. Made of a synthetic polymer chemically associated with super paste, these crystals can assimilate 400 times their weight in water, and then slowly discharge it back into their atmosphere. They look like crisp gelatin when fully hydrated.

They are used to monitor water use in agriculture and gardening, and to protect plants from drying out completely between watering. Similarly, the addition to a casing layer of only a small amount of water crystals would serve to keep it hydrated and reduce the need for steady misting. A single flush of mushrooms will ransack a considerable amount of water from the casing and substratum, and these crystals can give your cultures an extra degree of protection from drying out. Despite being a synthetic substance, water crystals have been tested and shown to be non-harmful and kindhearted to the environment. We absolutely convert to carbon dioxide and water after some time. We have even been experimentally tested for protection when used in growing mushrooms. Catch mushrooms (Agaricus bisporus) grown in their presence have not been shown to corrupt or introduce the gel's chemical constituents.

The crystals come in two assortments: ones made from sodium or others made from potassium. Since significant levels of sodium are harmful to numerous fungi, make certain to get the kind made from potassium. Because the crystals debase when heated, they should be added in the wake of disinfecting or sanitizing the casing soil. While a few growers recommend sanitizing casing soils before use to limit contaminations, we have found this progression pointless as long as the components are kept perfect and dry in the first place. Nonetheless, in the event that you need to be extra careful or you find that you do experience difficulty with contamination in your casing, a brisk sanitization may help. A basic method for sanitizing small quantities uses a microwave oven. Simply place the sodden, Prepared box soil in a heat-proof container or bag (wide oven bags, the kind used to cook turkeys, or large plastic cooler bags are ideal) and microwave it on high for about 15 minutes. Make sure the bag or bottle is left unsealed to avoid blasting. Enable the bag to sit for 10 minutes, then microwave for another 15 minutes afterwards. If you do not have a microwave, you can also sterilize it at 15 psi for 45 minutes in a pressure cooker or prepare it for 2 hours in a 3500 oven. Before using allow to cool absolutely. You may need to add more water to restore the casing soil to field capacity, as it will certainly force some moisture off after heating. We've provided three simple casing recipes, just to give you a sense of the varieties used and to leverage the resources that you might have readily available.

While they are all similarly effective in cultivating P cubensis, for a number of reasons we prefer the pure vermiculite formula. It is incredibly simple, for example. Coarse vermiculite is easy to remove from the base of the harvested mushrooms, in contrast to other casing materials. Vermiculite is created by a high-heat process, so it is exceptionally clean, completely contamination-resistant and does not need to be sanitized before I use. Most significantly, because vermiculite is an inorganic substance, it does not give the fungus any sustenance. Accordingly, overlay, a condition in which the casing is over colonized by mycelium and tightly' locked together, occurs with its use infrequently. Note: The dust from inhaled vermiculite is considered to be toxic to the lungs. The residual veil of a painter should be worn for health and wellbeing when it is first opened and played with. It avoids discharging dust when the vermiculite is moistened and is never risky again.

### Casing Soil Recipes

(All formulas are given on a by volume proportion.)

✓   Pure Vermiculite

- ✓ 10 parts coarse vermiculite
- ✓ '/2 section gypsum (CazSo4)
- ✓ 1/2 section chalk (CaCo3)
- ✓ Peat Moss Casing
- ✓ 10 parts peat moss
- ✓ 1/2 section gypsum (CazSo4)
- ✓ '/2 section chalk (CaCo3)
- ✓ "50/50" Mix
- ✓ 5 parts peat moss
- ✓ 5 parts coarse vermiculite
- ✓ 1/2 section gypsum (Ca2So,)
- ✓ 1/2 section chalk (CaCo3)

To every one of these formulas, you may add 1/2-teaspoon water crystals per liter or quart of casing soil. Always add these after any discretionary heat treatment. Regardless of which recipe you choose to use, the method of preparation is similar to that used in the PF Tek to bring the material to field capacity. Despite the fact that colonized substrates and casing soils are less dependent upon contamination than prior stages of growth, it is always a good plan to wear gloves and keep your workplace, tools, and containers as clean as could be expected under the circumstances.

1. Completely mix all the fixings together in a large, alcohol-sterilized container.

2. Save approximately 10 percent of this mixture.

3. Add water to the rest of it is saturated, and you simply begin to see free flowing water.

4. Add back the held dry mixture. In the event that appropriately moistened, pressing a

handful of the soil should yield a couple of drops of water. Sterilize or sanitize whenever desired and permit to cool completely. Test an example to make sure that it remains adequately moistened and add water if necessary.

5. Add water crystals Ch tsp per liter/quart), whenever desired.

6. Apply the casing a little at once to the substratum, thereby making the layer as even as reasonably expected. To hold the framework open and breezy stop pushing it hard. The last layer should have a thickness from 1/2 inch to 1 inch.

The container should be placed immediately under fruiting conditions, inside a bag or enclosure underneath the lights after the casing layer has been applied. Mist it gently and regularly using a hand sprayer filled with a solution of 0.3% peroxide (1 section 3% H2O2 combined with 9 parts water), set to produce a mist as fine as might be required under the circumstances. The water requirements of the fungus are negligible during the case colonization stage and spraying on more than one occasion per day should be sufficient to offset any loss due to vanishing. Be careful not to water it too vigorously or too deeply. Watering the layer of the casing gently and often is better, as opposed to soaking it at the same time which may appear to mat it down. The mycelium will begin to infiltrate the layer of the casing before long, jabbing up through it in places where it is thinner than others. Apply additional quantities of moistened casing soil for fixing these spots with a clean knife, so that colonization of the entire layer can proceed as equally as planned under the circumstances.

Overlay forming mycelium within the layer of the casing. Small amounts of additional casing soil can fill in the denser growth areas to allow even growth across the entire sheet. It is generally best if primordia form deep within the casing layer as opposed to on top of it, to prevent overlay issues. Overlay occurs when vegetative (i.e., non-fruiting) mycelium is allowed to colonize the entire layer of the casing, which at this point turns out to be firmly bonded. Water and gases are impervious to an overlaid casing dirt, and the mycelium within it bites the dust before long.

The most ideal way to avoid overlay is to start fruiting immediately in the wake of casing, and to make sure that the ideal conditions for fruiting are present from the start. Overlay is destined to occur when the air is stuffy, humid, and the greater part of all, excessively warm. Fruitbody inception occurs when the mycelium in the casing senses a temperature and humidity contrast between the substrate and the encompassing atmosphere.

As it grows from the substrate into the casing, it eventually arrives at a boundary where moisture and temperature levels fall, implying to the mycelium that the vegetative stage is finished, and the time has come to begin fruiting. Exceptionally high humidity and warmth prevent the acknowledgment of this boundary, so the mycelium just keeps directly on growing, and because it has no place else to go, it just grows over itself, creating overlay.

By setting the freshly cased substrate under lights immediately, misting normally, permitting sufficient ventilation, and taking care not to overheat your growing area, the culture will fruit when it is ready, and overlay won't occur.

### Scratching

When the casing layer is applied, it is ideal to avoid touching or manipulating it, so you don't harm the delicate primordia or present contaminants. Be that as it may, in spite of your earnest attempts, there may in any case be events when you experience overlay. Provided that this is true, you can safeguard a casing layer by scratching it. To scratch a casing layer, simply take a clean metal fork, sterilize it with scouring alcohol, and tenderly scratch the casing down to the top of the substrate layer (make an effort not to touch the casing with your hands as you do as such). Extricate it up however much as could be expected, while maintaining an even depth.

Mist the scratched casing lightly and permit it to hatch in your fruiting chamber as in the past. In the event that you are scratching more than one container, always sterilize your fork after everyone to avoid spreading concealed contaminants. The mycelium in more established overlaid casings is potentially already dead and conveys a higher likelihood of contamination. Along these lines, this method is best when done as ahead of schedule as conceivable after the issue is discovered.

## Contamination

While casing soils themselves are generally resistant to contamination, the mycelium itself is less along these lines, especially as its ages. Typically, contamination sets in simply after a few flushes of mushrooms have been harvested and the substrate is almost depleted of supplements. If contamination occurs from the get-go in the casing stage, it is most likely a sign of an issue inhabitant in the substrate or the casing soil itself, and the culture is best discarded for starting with a clean one.

As somewhere else, endeavoring to "spare" a polluted culture is generally not worth the disappointment, and is just likely to spread the contamination to different containers. There is one type of contamination remarkable to casing soils that you may every so often experience. This is Dactylium dendroides, also called "cobweb mold," for its wispy, web-like appearance. It begins as small pinpoints of fine, white fluff on top of the casing layer, and rapidly grows to cover it completely. Cobweb mold is handily spread between containers at the slightest air unsettling influence, so debased cultures ought to be removed when they are discovered. Whenever permitted to proliferate, it will eventually assault and overview any mushrooms or primordia in the container, decreasing them to a vile mush.

Once in a while beginning growers will mistake the underlying growth of mushroom mycelium into the casing layer for cobweb mold. Genuine cobweb mold grows as a fluffy layer on top of the casing soil, while the mushroom mycelium rises through it from underneath. In addition, mushroom mycelium, while it might look wispy from the outset, will immediately thicken in appearance. The occurrence of cobweb mold can be prevented by maintaining satisfactory air exchange inside the fruiting container, avoiding over the top humidity levels, and purifying the casing soil preceding application.

# CHAPTER 8

## *Fruiting and harvesting*

Many other cultivated species of mushrooms need a drop in temperature or an expansion in humidity to improve fruiting, but P cubensis does not. Thanks to a humid environment, appropriate exchange of gas, and ample light, P cubensis can yield precipitous fruit, often before the mycelium has penetrated the surface of the case layer. A variety of growers suggest extensive misting or fanning systems and cold stunning the crop by freezing it in a refrigerator overnight to start fruiting, but we consider these methods superfluous. Because the strain being cultivated is a fiery fruit tree and its essential requirements have been met, it should survive.

In this way, your efforts are best spent on discovering a good fruiting strain at a timely time, as opposed to working hard to get a poor one to fruit. In case you are familiar with the "PF Tek," you should already find much of this section commonplace. You should see primordia, little mushrooms at their most immature stage, starting to form in a few days to about fourteen days after casing. Ideally, they will grow inside the casing layer and will not be visible until smaller than expected mushrooms are already shaped all around. They tend to grow incredibly fast when they have accomplished this size (around 1 h cm) and may seem to arrive practically overnight at full size. As they grow, water will be drawn from the secret substratum and casing layer, so make sure that misting increases differently (always taking care not to overwater).

### Harvesting

When the mushroom has arrived at a fitting size for productive spore dispersal (for the most part somewhere close to 3 inches and 6 inches in tallness), it stops growing and its cap augments, opening to expose its gills to the atmosphere. The best time to harvest your mushrooms is only before this point, when the veil is stretched however not broken, since after this point the mushrooms will never again put on any real weight. In addition, you don't need spores falling onto your casing soil and containers.

Given the cosmic numbers of spores produced by a solitary mushroom, this can make a serious chaos; in addition, the gases discharged by sprouting spores can potentially hinder further fruiting. The easiest way to tell when a mushroom is preparing to open is to give close consideration to the partial veil, the thin protective film that covers the gills. At first, the cap is completely enrolled (looking a lot of like those good old globe-on-a-shaft streetlamps), and the partial veil is covered up. As the cap starts to expand, the veil develops as a roundabout, light-colored band around the bottom hemisphere of the cap.

When the cap begins to flatten out, the partial veil gets stretched past its ability to expand and begins to tear, pulling away from the outer edges of the gills. Eventually, the partial veil separates from the cap entirely and its leftovers stay joined to the stipe in a skirt-like ring, known as an annulus.

Ideally, you need to pick your mushrooms when the partial veil is visible, or at the latest, when the veil begins to break. Harvesting the mushrooms is as basic as getting a handle on them at the base and bending tenderly while pulling up into the clouds from the casing. Any piece of the mushroom that remaining parts in the casing will rot, so take care to remove everything, down to the base of the stipe, utilizing forceps or a pair of clean chopsticks if fundamental. Do whatever it takes not to touch the casing layer legitimately with your hands and take extraordinary care not to harm less-created mushrooms or primordia close by.

Sometimes, it is difficult to avoid upsetting or evacuating close by mushrooms when harvesting. Right now, is smarter to remove these "babies" as well, instead of leaving them behind. Upsetting them often cuts off their association with the substrate and they stop growing and eventually rot. Don't stress a lot over the periodic loss, since whatever vitality the culture would have expended on these fruits will be occupied to the following flush. Generally, a considerable lot of vermiculite will be adhered to the base of the harvested mushrooms, leaving behind a divot in the casing layer. When you are done harvesting, simply fill these holes with fresh, appropriately moistened casing soil, mist altogether, and return the container to the fruiting area.

During the period immediately following a harvest, increment misting recurrence and quantity essentially, so as to replace the substantial amount of water removed from the casing in the harvested mushrooms. Every container should produce three to five harvests, or flushes, of mushrooms with a week or so of recovery time between each flush.

Generally, the initial barely any flushes are the most plenteous. After the fourth or fifth flush, the substrate will be exhausted, the mass of substrate will have noticeably shrunk, and the number of mushrooms that form will be insignificant. Now, the containers ought to be discarded, since the mycelium in them will begin to kick the bucket. Weak or dead mycelium is likely to get debased with molds, which could then spread to your healthy cultures.

### Cleaning the Harvest

Over the long haul, it is simpler and much better hoping to clean off the mushroom stems when they are fresh as opposed to after they have been dried. Any casing soil staying on the base of harvested mushrooms can be removed by delicately scratching it off with a blade in a descending movement.

### Yields and Biological Efficiency

Exactly what number of mushrooms would it be a good idea for you to hope to harvest from a specific amount of substrate? To address this inquiry, we have to allude to the idea of Biological Efficiency, or B.E., a term created by the business mushroom industry. The biological efficiency of a mushroom is its characteristic ability to change over substrate into mushrooms; A B.E. of 1 00% means either a 25% change of the wet mass of the substrate into fresh mushrooms, or a 1 0% transformation of the dry substrate into dry mushrooms. At the end of the day, at 1 00% B.E., 1 00 g dry wheat berries could be relied upon to produce around 1 00 g fresh mushrooms, or 1 0 9 dries.

P cubensis is a genuinely vigorous species, and commonly accomplishes yields a lot higher than 1 00% B.E. (maybe as much as 200%, or a 20 g for every 1 00 g dry substrate). Notwithstanding, it is generally recommended that you not have a go at extracting each and every mushroom from your containers, and instead start fresh ones. As a rule, after the third or fourth flush the number of fruits produced will greatly decay and the culture will get vulnerable to contamination, which could then handily spread to healthy cultures close by.

### After the Harvest

### Preserving Mushrooms

You can store fresh mushrooms in the refrigerator for up to seven days, without rotting or losing power. For example, they should be put in a breathable container, a paper (not plastic) bag, or a sealable plastic container fastened with a paper towel, slightly ajar to the lid. If you need to store your mushrooms for longer periods, you can maintain them in one way or another, as psilocybin and its related mixtures oxidize easily and become inactive when exposed to the atmosphere. The easiest and best preservation tool is to dry out. Dry psilocybin mushrooms, kept from light, heat, and moisture, can maintain their potency for a long, even years. Gradually drying the fresh mushrooms under gentle heat (1 10 ° F or below) until the "cracker" is firm, and no longer supple. Then put them, for example, in a sealed container, a zippered cooler bag or, even better, a heat-sealed bag for storing food.

Before sealing it, however much air as required should be expelled from the container. Singular bags should be put in an optional sealed container for added protection before freezing. If space is at a premium, after drying, the mushrooms may be powdered in a zest plant or coffee processor, but they will not maintain their potency as long as they are kept intact, because their chemical components will be exposed to the atmosphere for a greater amount. A kitchen food dehydrator makes an excellent drying apparatus for mushrooms, especially one that has accurate temperature control and a circulating ventilator. The best models circle warm air in a flat way which results in all racks being dried. By building a wooden box with removable, sliding wire screen racks and an I SO-watt radiant light bulb at its base as a heat source, a makeshift food dehydrator can also be handy designed. On the other hand, mushrooms may be dried by putting them over a radiator overnight in a warm oven or on a rack. Make sure to use gentle heat, 110 ° F (4Y C) or underneath, whatever drying system you use. At higher temperatures dried mushrooms will be harsh tasting and substantially less active.

### Spore Printing

Freshly harvested mushrooms being stacked into a food dehydrator. Spore printing, like tissue cloning, is a method of preserving the hereditary makeup of your cultures. Spores are the result of sexual propagation, which means that a spore print will contain a wide range of genotypes. As in human propagation, every individual spore (or "child") will be made from some irregular blend of characters from every one of its two parent cores. Carefully, a spore print will never contain the very same hereditary qualities as the mushroom it originated from (unlike tissue cloning, which will).

By the by, Psilocybe mushroom species are regularly very steady starting with one age then onto the next, and the great greater part of spores in a print will behave indistinguishably from their parents. Spore prints can remain viable for quite a long time if they are kept from light, heat, and moisture. In this way, they represent a form of protection in case a cloned strain loses life or is lost through and through.

### Making a Spore Print

1.  To take a spore print, you will require a mushroom on which the cap is flat, and the

gills are fully opened. (This is the one example when you should let the mushroom create past the globe-on-a-stick organize and permit the partial veil to begin to break before harvesting.) As with cloning, pick just the largest, most powerful specimens for spore printing, and make multiple prints at whatever point conceivable.

2. With a clean, sharp blade, cut the stem of the mushroom just beneath where it connects to the cap, so when placed face down, it will be raised a millimeter or two over the printing surface. Make the cut as clean and flat as conceivable so as to give a level and stable base. With the tip of the blade, remove any hints of the partial veil from the gills. Avoid touching the gills straightforwardly.

3. Prints can be developed on paper, glass microscope slides, or aluminum foil. Of these, glass or foil are ideal, because they can be sterilized by cleaning them down with alcohol and drying before use, and their smooth surface texture permits the spores to be effortlessly removed with an inoculation loop later on. Clean plastic Petri dishes work pleasantly also, gave the cap is sufficiently small to fit serenely within them. Take a few prints on a solitary sheet of foil, leaving abundant space I between each cap, with the goal that the foil can be collapsed over e print for capacity. I f utilizing slides, you will most likely need to use a few to contain an entire cap.

4.  Sterilize the printing surface with alcohol and permit to dry.

5.  Place the cap face down on the printing material and cover it with a transformed container to maintain a humid environment and limit air flows.

6.  Within a couple of hours, the cap ought to have stored its print onto the foil. Slower delivering specimens can be left overnight to create a denser print, if fundamental.

7.  The finished print ought to be sealed to limit contamination. In the event that utilizing foil or paper, cut out the print, and crease clean foil over it, taking care not to press directly on the spores beneath. Seal the edges by collapsing them over. If you use glass microscope slides, cover the print with a clean blank slide, and tape the edges.

8.  Place the prints inside zippered stockpiling bags and imprint them with the date and some other important information. Spore prints ought to be stored in a detect that is away from light, moisture, and heat, however, ought not be refrigerated or solidified. All around preserved spore prints can remain viable for a long time.

# CHAPTER 9

## *Outdoor cultivation*

Outside mushroom cultivation offers a number of important advantages over growing inside. When an outside garden bed has betin set up, it will fruit every year for quite a while, until the substrate has been fully consumed. By intermittently adding fresh wood chips to the mixture, or by creating another bed close by and utilizing a portion of the first substrate as inoculum, the life of a bed can be extended uncertainly. Such beds require practically no maintenance past keeping them damp during the drier, hotter months of the mid-year. Since wood chips are modest, and can even sometimes be had for free, outside cultivation is economical.

Wood based substrates are far less inclined to colonization by bacteria and molds, so they can be handled openly, unafraid of contamination. Finally, since they can be handily incorporated into pretty much any obscure, off the beaten path garden area, outside mushroom gardens are definitely more discreet and low profile than some other mushroom cultivation method. In spite of the fact that the substrate colonization and fruiting stages of open-air cultivation require next to no maintenance, the early stages are pretty much indistinguishable from those required for P cubensis cultivation. Spores are developed utilizing the cardboard plate method, and the subsequent mycelium is grown out on agar in Petri dishes, and afterward transferred to sterile grain. When the grain spawn is fully colonized, it is used to immunize small quantities of sterilized wood-based substrate. This wood-based spawn is used to immunize a large quantity of wood chips, which are then utilized to create the last bed. When the fruiting substrate is fully colonized, fruitings initiate when the surrounding temperatures fall into the 40° F range, from mid-October until early winter in northern North America. Flushes show up once at regular intervals or something like that, as long as temperature remains consistent.

### Temperature Requirements

P cubensis and the different lignicolous (wood loving) Psilocybes will fruit outside just if your nearby temperatures drop into the forties every harvest time and stay there for a few weeks or more. In the event that you live in Florida or southern California, you will sadly need to adhere to growing P cubensis) or think about moving some place less soothing.

## About Wood Substrates

The mycelium of the "wood-loving" species will grow readily on pretty much anything derived from trees, inasmuch as it is either made from hardwoods, or derived from softwoods that have been stripped of their aromatic constituents, like most paper items. With regards to fruiting, they are progressively specific, and will just do as such from a mixture of hardwood chips and sawdust.

In any case, you have a wide variety of substrate alternatives with regards to the pre-fruiting stages of cultivation. Wood-based substrates are naturally resistant to attack by molds and bacteria, so they need not be sterilized before use. Substrates that are readily consumed by certain fungi, while resistant to attack by different organisms, are known as specific for those species. Wood is basically made out of cellulose and lignin. Lignin particles are long, cross-linked chains of phenolic natural mixes. The bonds that make up lignin are incredibly chemically steady, which gives wood its trademark hardness and longevity. As a log consuming in your fireplace will affirm, there is a great arrangement of vitality contained in wood, yet it is bound firmly within the lignin latticework and isn't effortlessly gotten to by most organisms. In fact, the main organisms that can break down and expend lignin are sure species of fungi.

The fungi that have the fundamental proteins to do so are called "lignicolous" or "wood-possessing" fungi, a gathering that incorporates the caramel-cap Psilocybes. The selectivity of wood substrates for lignicolous fungi is the thing that makes them extensively simpler to handle than materials like grain. One intriguing feature of these species is that cultures gathered from the wild or from healthy cultivated beds are amazingly versatile, capable of flourishing under conditions that "virgin" pure spawn cultures would not survive. This is because introduction to different difficulties invigorates a living being to express its full capabilities.

Virgin cultures that have grown distinctly on sterile media made of straightforward components have not very many of their chemical creating qualities actuated. Free-living organisms, then again, have needed to contend day by day with a wide range of different species, and have by need built up the capacity to survive in their presence. Such "acclimated" cultures assembled from the wild are shockingly hearty.

They will grow readily on unsterilized substrates, and often appear to improve on "dirty" substrates than on clean ones. Obviously, in the event that you are starting from a spore print, this fact will be of little use to you, in any event from the outset. You despite everything need to use sterile methods in the early stages of the procedure: from cardboard plates to agar, at that point to grain, lastly to sterilized wood. Be that as it may, in the event that you are lucky to approach an already settled bed, either because you live where these mushrooms grow in the wild, or because you or somebody you know experiences already gone to the difficulty of creating one, you can do without clean methods out and out, and simply transfer mycelium to fresh substrate to create another bed.

# CHAPTER 10

## *The chemistry of Psilocybe mushrooms*

The chemical compounds present in Psilocybe mushrooms are a group of similar tryptamines, substances consisting of an indole ring and an amine bound to a two-carbon chain. If in this chapter you find the actual chemistry a little esoteric, don't stress too much. The essential take-away lesson is this: these compounds are all closely related to the natural amino acid L-tryptophan from which they are produced by the fungus, and to serotonin (5-hydroxytryptamine), a major mammalian neurotransmitter that helps to explain their pharmacological effects on humans.] Psilocin and its phosphate ester psilocybin are the most common compounds found in these fungi, while bae Psilocybin is quickly converted into psilocin by eliminating its phosphate group in the body, making the two compounds more or less identical in effects and potency after their different molecular weights are taken into consideration. The psychoactive effects of baeocystin and norbaeocystin in isolation are not well understood but there is some evidence to suggest modulating the psychoactive effects of psilocybin and psilocybin. Their existence in varying amounts may help explain common anecdotal reports of subjective differences from one species of Psilocybe mushroom to another. In the first place, almost nothing definitive is known about why these chemicals are present in those mushrooms, due to the various legal barriers to public scientific study of these mushroom species.

Nature seldom does anything without a practical purpose, especially when the action is energetically expensive, as it is here for sure. Such compounds have to serve some evolutionary advantage for the survival of these species; otherwise, for example, the resources which go into synthesizing them would be better spent on making more spores or larger fruit bodies. One might be tempted to suggest that these molecules guarantee the mushroom species ' survival because their existence allows people to grow and spread them for their psychoactive effects. Such logic, however, gives human beings far more credit than they owe, as these fungi just got along fine tor millions of years without our help. During their constant struggle to compete and survive in the natural environment, the chemicals they produce must have had a certain important purpose. Many organisms produce chemicals in their environment which have some positive or negative ecological effects on other species. Such compounds are often referred to as "secondary" metabolites, since they are not known to have any primary effect on the internal functioning of the organism itself, but are better considered as allochemicals, compounds whose effect is intended to influence other organisms. Allelochemicals can serve three roles that are interrelated: semiotic, competitive and/or symbiotic. Semiotic compounds give the receiver a signal to come closer or stay away. Many flowers ' powerful scents are meant to attract pollinating insects or animals, while other organisms discourage foraging from the bitter compounds in other plant leaves. Competitive chemicals can be defensive or offensive at once, or both.

A honeybee's sting does no lasting harm to its victim, but it does all the same teach a valuable lesson in avoidance. On the other hand, that of the hornet or wasp aims primarily at killing its insect prey. Symbiotic allochemicals give both producer and recipient mutual benefit: the Colibri receives nourishing nectar in exchange for (unwittingly) pollen spreading from one flower to another. It is not known what allochemicals function psilocybin might serve for the fungi which produce it, but it is most likely defensive. It can help prevent other organisms from competing for resources or feeding on the tender and nutrient-rich hyphae while exploring the substrate environment. Maybe these chemicals kill or inhibit the growth of snails, slugs, or worms.] They may also possess antibiotic properties, helping prevent bacteria or other fungi from attacking the fungus.

The fact that they are produced in a lot greater concentrations in the fruit bodies than in the bare mycelium lends support to the possibility that they serve a cautious capacity: if the objective of the mushroom life cycle is to produce and discharge whatever number spores as could reasonably be expected, the fruits require the greatest protection from attack. Regardless of whether these molecules are not synthesized by the fungus for the "purpose" of empowering a progressing relationship with human creatures, there is no doubt that they do effetely affect the human brain. It could be contended that these effects are unplanned, yet not circumstantial: human creatures developed in a similar environment as worms, bacteria, and fungi, and are made up from a similar fundamental chemical and biological structure blocks. Numerous organisms have tryptamine-like molecules in them; however, they are firmly related chemically, the capacities they serve are often as various as the organisms themselves. Researcher like to use the lock-and-key metaphor to depict the activity of chemicals on biological systems: when the key (the chemical) is embedded into the lock (the receptors on or inside the cells of the living being), some effect occurs. Because all organisms advanced from a typical progenitor, the number of such chemical "keys" is constrained, while their effects are most certainly not. What happens when you put psilocybin into a slug or into a human depends upon the area and the capacity of the receptors with which it associates. Precisely how psilocybin produces the effects that it does on the human brain is still particularly a puzzle, both because of the profound intricacy of the organ and the legal limitations placed on the study of psychedelic molecules. By the by, it is believed that its essential effect is mostly the consequence of its cooperation with certain serotonin receptors.

Neurobiologists allude to two nonexclusive types of dynamic molecules: agonists and foes. An agonist ties to a receptor with a similar effect as the real neurotransmitter, while an adversary blocks the effect of the neurotransmitter. Coming back to our lock-and-key metaphor, an agonist is a key that fits and turns the lock, however maybe with pretty much efficiency than the neurotransmitter itself, while a rival only sticks in the lock, preventing the real key from getting in. Psilocybin and related molecules are thought to be serotonin agonists. They tie to receptors and follow up on them much like serotonin does, yet with a slightly extraordinary proclivity. While the effect at every individual receptor site may be inconspicuous, their general effect on the human mind is obviously profound.

Psilocybin Safety Given their powerful psychological effects on humans and their theoretical functions as defensive allochemicals, one might reasonably wonder if the compounds found in Psilocybe mushrooms could be toxic to human health in any way. There is in fact no evidence to suggest they are poisonous at all. First of all, they are unlikely to be toxic, as they have such a long history of human use with no single death attributed.

Moreover, these molecules were subjected to traditional toxicology tests many times, which proved to be quite innocuous.

Psilocybin has an LD-50(or 50 percent lethal dose) of about 250mg / kg in rats and mice, which means you need to give 250 milligrams of psilocybin to the test animals for every kilogram of body weight to kill half of them. Approximately, what this means for humans is that the average adult SO-kilogram male would need to ingest 22 grams of pure psilocybin, or about 500 grams of dried Psilocybe cubensis mushrooms, to earn a 50 percent chance of dying! By comparison, caffeine, widely considered a benign human drug, has an LD-50 of 1 92mg / kg in rats, making it as "toxic" as psilocybin about 1-5 times.

# CHAPTER 11

## *The Psilocybe mushroom experience*

We assume that you would not experience gone to all the difficulty to figure out how to grow psilocybin-containing mushrooms without some previous direct experience with their psychoactive effects, and some comprehension on the most proficient method to use them. In the event that you are curious about their effects, we conm1end your excitement and assurance for having come this far on the unimportant guarantee of the delights and ponders that these mushrooms can uncover. We assume that before you push off onto these huge, still generally strange, and always secretive waters, you will have done your homework.

Counsel with other people who have gone before you, either in person, on the web, or in print.! The more you know before you set off, the better prepared you will be for the secrets you will experience, and the more fortunes you will have the option to convey with you on your arrival. We have a couple of recommendations for how to make the greater part of the mushroom experience. Obviously, you should think about such exhortation while taking other factors into consideration since, as always, your mileage may shift.

**Fresh versus Dry**

Since all things considered, your cultivation undertakings will give definitely a greater number of mushrooms than you might require at any one time, you will likely dry them for long-term stockpiling and sometime in the future. Psilocybe mushrooms can be ingested fresh, however there are two factors to consider if you choose to do as such. To begin with, fresh mushrooms are approximately 90% water by weight, so you should multiply the weight of your dosage by a factor of 10 when utilizing fresh mushrooms.

In addition, numerous people (your modest creators included) find fresh mushrooms impressively less edible than dried ones for some unknown explanation. More than once have we eaten freshly picked mushrooms to find ourselves affiicted with issues, heartburn, and general discomfort for a great part of the journey. Drying them appears to dispose of whatever factor produces these effects. One way to avoid acid reflux when utilizing fresh mushrooms is to make an implantation from them (as described underneath) and discard the solids in the wake of soaking. In the event that you do choose to eat fresh specimens, make sure they are clean, firm, and as of late picked. More established, delicate fruits can harbor bacteria and ought to be discarded.

## Dosage

Recommending a dosage system for mushroom ingestion is convoluted by the great variability in the potency of mushrooms, both among various species, and between strains or flushes of similar species. In addition to the great variety in potency among various mushrooms, there is likewise an undeniable and often wide variety in individual sensitivity to psilocybin. What may be a threshold dose (at the end of the day, the most reduced conceivable amount expected to feel any effect at all) for one person might be a whopper for another. It is very important that every person be all around familiar with their own sensitivity before exploring different avenues regarding a new example or dosage. If all else fails, it is always best to decide in favor of alert; you can always take increasingly next time around, or much later on, after the effects of the primary dose have made themselves fully felt. (An hour and a half is typically adequately long to hold up before taking a supporter dose.) One important influence on individual sensitivity is body mass; because the drug is distributed pretty much uniformly all through the body after ingestion, a heavier person will require a larger dose to accomplish a similar effect as somebody of small stature. Thus, recommended dosages of pure mixes are given as milligrams per kilogram of body mass (mg per kg). One kilogram is equal to 2.2 pounds.

## Dosage levels

### Low Dose: 5-1 0 mg alkaloids

At this level, the mushrooms have quite recently started to make themselves felt, creating a gentle, indistinct adjusted state, not unlike an "up" marijuana high. The body feels stimulated and the mind alert. Senses and perceptions are heightened. Colors may appear to be more splendid and progressively striking, music and sounds often appear to be increasingly particular and fresh, tastes are enhanced, etc.

While perceptions of the outer world are lightly adjusted, genuine sound or visual hallucinations are unlikely to occur at this dosage. Such low doses are agreeable to use in open settings, for example, workmanship museums or musical shows, since one's outward appearance will be sufficiently ordinary to avoid pulling in undesirable attention from strangers. This is likewise an excellent dose level for daytime investigation and contemplatory' of the natural world. £ The effects at this level generally commence within 30 minutes, and last from 2-4 hours.

### Medium Dose: 1 2-25 mg alkaloids

At this level, both shut and open-peered toward visual hallucinations can emerge. At first, and at the lower range of the medium dosage, these are basically exceptionally colored, striking geometric examples, not unlike elaborate, living Oriental mats. Synesthesis, where at least two senses cross or cover are normal at this level. Tastes, smells, touch, music and different sounds can enhance and synergize with the visuals in amazing and astounding ways, and the other way around. At slightly higher doses, conceptual dreams can give way to progressively pictorial images, both recognizable and strange. With adequate experience and solace with these dosage levels, one can wander out into the natural world, to great effect, yet we recommend avoiding contact with strangers at whatever point conceivable. The effects at this level generally starts within 30 minutes, and last from 3-5 hours.

### High Dose: 30-40 mg alkaloids

At these doses, the sky really is the limit. Terence McKenna alluded to such amounts as "chivalrous doses," since each experience is definitely a journey into uncharted waters. What you will find we can't state, since the experience will be exceptionally personal and always particular. We do anyway recommend that you make sure to find yourself in agreeable and protected settings before you begin, free from interruptions and undesirable shocks. Quiet darkness, alone or with a guide is ideal for such voyages. Don't think about wandering out into the "real world" at this dose level. You presumably won't have the option to stand up, considerably less stroll with any amount of coordination anyway. At high doses, the mushroom experience generally commences within 30 minutes, and endures from 5-7 hours.

### Higher Doses

We don't recommend doses much past 0.5mg/kg, in any event, for the most experienced and valiant explorer. After this point the theory of consistent losses sets in, and the experience turns out to be longer and progressively intense without fundamentally being all the more fulfilling. Psilocybe alkaloids are very benevolent to human health and it is basically difficult to take an "overdose," at any rate one that is truly harmful to human health. In the event that you find you have taken more than you ought to have, coincidentally or something else, have confidence that, in spite of the intensity of the experience, you will most likely survive. Indeed, even at very high doses, the experience will last no longer than 8 hours, with the most intense part over far sooner than that.

### Monoamine Oxidase (MAO) Inhibitors and Psilocybe Alkaloids

If you are as of now taking monoamine oxidase medications of any kind, you ought not to ingest psilocybin (or any psychedelics, for that matter.) These drugs are intended to deactivate the human chemical system answerable for the digestion of numerous drugs and basic food poisons. With MAO idle, aggravates the body would somehow or another corrupt can have unpredictable and potentially perilous effects. In the event that you are taking MAO inhibitors for depression (their most basic sign), you should hold up until you have stopped taking them before exploring different avenues regarding psilocybin. Another psychedelic, the Amazonian blend ayahuasca, deliberately joins a MAO inhibitor from the vine Bannisteriopsis caapi with a tryptamine-containing plant to produce its effects. Some smart "psychonauts" have used this model to create a "mycohuasca" by joining Psilocybemushrooms with B. caapi or other MAO-repressing plants, dramatically potentiating and adjusting their effects. We don't recommend doing as such, however in the event that you choose to try different things with something like this yourself, it would be ideal if you be careful and, as always, get your work done.

### Tolerance

At the point when psilocybin is used more than once every week, tolerance generally occurs. The specific causes behind this phenomenon are not surely known, yet the general effect is that the brain turns out to be incidentally desensitized to a specific drug after every presentation. While tolerance to psilocybin can be overwhelmed by essentially expanding the dose, it is ideal to simply hold up at any rate a week between voyages to give the brain (just as your mind) a chance to come back to baseline.

### Methods of ingestion

A great many people simply bite and swallow the dried mushrooms. For the individuals who find them to some degree not exactly agreeable, it is simple enough to make an extract, since the alkaloids in Psilocybe mushrooms are freely dissolvable in both ethanol and hot water. Regardless of what method of ingestion you use, it is prudent to wait for a least 6 hours before utilizing Psilocybe mushrooms, to minimize heartburn and to expand retention of the alkaloids.

## Mushroom Tea

Simply make a pot of your preferred home-grown tea utilizing one and one-half cups of water per person, preferably utilizing aromatic herbs and flavors, for example, mint, cinnamon, or cloves to help cover the taste of the mushrooms and to quiet the stomach. In the wake of soaking the tea for 10 minutes or somewhere in the vicinity, pour it into a subsequent pot containing the imperative amount of fresh or dried mushrooms. Cover this and permit to soak for in any event one hour, mixing every so often. Strain and pour into the suitable number of teacups. The remaining mushroom solids might be eaten, yet this is generally redundant, since the vast majority of the alkaloids will have infused into the tea. High temperatures will quickly corrupt alkaloids, so the soaking fluid ought to never be permitted to boil once the mushrooms have been added. If the tea isn't used immediately, it ought to be refrigerated. When prepared, mushroom tea ought to be used within 48 hours.

### Alcohol Extract

For a longer enduring preparation, think about making an extract. Squashed or powdered mushrooms can be soaked in high-proof alcohol (1 50-proof or greater, for example, rum or Ever clear, utilizing 25-50 milliliters of alcohol for each dose. Subsequent to soaking for 3 days or longer, the extract can be filtered or tapped and stored for a while or longer without extensive loss of potency.

# CHAPTER 12

## *How to grow your own psychedelic mushrooms*

I t is recommended to build your own fungi culture at home in case you need to be separate from the cache of fungi out in nature and the contributions from some smart shops in specific countries. There are different cultivation methods for each specie. The most cultivated psychedelic mushrooms are Psilocybe cubensis, sometimes called the "Mexican." The reason they are so popular is because under controlled conditions, they are very easy to grow. In Europe they have to be grown indoors. Then again there are various species that can grow outside effectively. Psilocybe cyanescens are local fungi that grow similarly on wood chips as does the Psilocybe azurescens. The methods of cultivating the two last once, however, are very special to the technique for growing Psilocybe cubensis.

In general, it's a little harder to grow your own fungi than cultivating your own weed. Before you start with the culture of the fungi you have to learn basic concepts and function precisely. The biggest problem is job sterile more often than not. If one starts planting, you know very quickly that crops of fungi are susceptible to bacteria and mold. Whether you are really working properly and sterilizing your glass with the culture can get infected even now. Don't get distracted by the boy! Observe just what you are doing and what has turned out badly. Attempt to make a profit from your mistake.

### Guidance to cultivate your own fungi Source:

The following technique was distributed without precedent for Seattle in September 1991 under the name PF TEK (Psilocybe Fanaticus technique). Around 1998 the greater part a million of models were available for use. The PF TEK is the most famous natural fungi grow technique in the world. This approved variant was adjusted to circumstance in Europe by the Stitching Perfect Fungi.

### One needs the following extras:

- ✓ Drug store
- ✓ Needles with needle protection
- ✓ Clean packed infusion needles
- ✓ Syringes and needles are just important when one needs to make its own spore's syringes
- ✓ Development market or hardware store
- ✓ Awl (or knitting needle)
- ✓ Drugstore
- ✓ Spiritus (70–80% volume alcohol)

- ✓ Small and bended line cuticle scissors or small scissors with small tip
- ✓ Antibacterial cleanser
- ✓ Spongy cotton
- ✓ Gardening shop
- ✓ Plant sprayer
- ✓ Perlit
- ✓ Vermikulit (corn size 0–3mm, grade nr. 2)
- ✓ Household article (market, store, health shop, etc)
- ✓ Tinfoil
- ✓ Autoclave
- ✓ Lighter
- ✓ Glasses with smooth sidewalls
- ✓ 15 watts-bulb
- ✓ Purple bug lamp or 370-nm-black light (Philips color 5)
- ✓ Kitchen fork
- ✓ Cooler
- ✓ Beaker
- ✓ Estimating scoop
- ✓ Translucent plastic bag
- ✓ Rice flour or brown rice
- ✓ Soup bowl
- ✓ Toilette paper
- ✓ Stationery shop
- ✓ Elastic groups
- ✓ Marker
- ✓ Sellotape
- ✓ Pressing film
- ✓ Pet shop
- ✓ Smaller than expected aquarium
- ✓ Thermometer for the aquarium

Besides, one ought to have a residue free room (for instance a big material closet or a not particularly used shower), a scratch plate, a seating convenience, a blowtorch and a cooler with freezers.

## 1 — Glasses

Deal with the surface of the glasses when you're picking. Along these lines, you'll have a substantially more open to harvesting process. More smaller glasses are superior to a ton of big size glasses. The reason accordingly is that there will happen contaminations occasionally.

### 1.1 One takes:

Appropriate glasses which are easy to upset like a cake tin. The glasses must not deform during the process of cooking out.

### 1.2 Glasses which were already used a couple of times

Reasonable glasses made out of white glass are jelly glasses up to 385 ml or preserving jars.

### 1.3 Plastic glasses and form

Sterilisable jars made out of heat-resistant plastic, for example, Polypropylene (PP) are functional. The name is often discovered in a small triangular image. They're modest, light and unbreakable, yet not offer handy to close.

### 1.4 Drinking glasses

Drinking glasses are additionally alright for cultivating. At the point when you use those as a tank, you'll use the tinfoil as a cover. When utilizing them there's a bigger chance of getting infected than when you're utilizing glasses with a screw-cap. At the point when you fix the foil with an elastic band and take a thicker layer of Vermiculite you can limit the risk.

## 2 Preparation of the soil and the process of sterilize

Fungi are more easy organisms than plants. They do not need any chlorophyll and along these lines acquire oxygen just as azotic from outside.

### 2.1.1 One takes:

Rice flour or brown rice (self-processed brown rice is superior to pre-packed rice flour)

- ✓ Medium coarse Vermiculite
- ✓ Glasses with smooth sidewalls
- ✓ Beaker
- ✓ Sellotape
- ✓ Awl or knitting needle
- ✓ Soup bowl
- ✓ Kitchen fork

### 2.1.2 Recipe for the preparation of the soil

A most extreme harvest will be accomplished when you use a 1/4 glass with brown rice flour, a 1/2 glass with medium coarse Vermiculite and a 1/4 glass with water.

### 2.2 Procedure for 320 ml glasses

If you use glasses with a plastic cover (or foil covered glasses) start with stage 3.

Screw the cover on the glass.

Sting four holes into the cover.

Scoop 160 ml of Vermiculite into the soup bowl.

Scoop 80 ml of rice flour over it.

Run over carefully 80 ml of water.

Mix everything appropriately until there is no dry rice flour any longer.

Mix the soil for every cultivation container individually. Along these lines, you avoid the creation of clusters.

Fill the classes freely.

Hit smoothly the bottom of the glass with your palm. Presently, shake the glass a little with the goal that the soil can spread similarly.

Clean the edge of the glass.

Presently put a little layer of dry Vermiculite over the soil.

In the event that there's any extra Vermiculite in the glass you can take it carefully out. In any case, don't press in any of it in the soil.

Stick the holes on the cover with the sellotape and make sure that potential air pockets are removed. Close the cover however not very tight.

### 2.3 Sterilize

In the principal period of the growth, the Myzel is truly defenseless for infections which can be caused by mold and bacteria. In the process of cooking out, the microorganisms will get slaughtered and their generation stopped.

### 2.3.1 One takes:

A pot with easy closable cover. At the bottom of the pot we have to have a framework which avoids that the glasses have contact with the bottom.

### 2.3.2 Procedure

Cook the glasses for one hour at around 100 degree Celsius. If you have a quick cooking pot you cook it for around 30 minutes at 120-degree celsius. The cover of the pot must be closed excellent. Something else, the soil will dry out. Look to it that no water interacts with the soil and take care that there's sufficient water in the pot.

### 2.4 Waiting time

Preserve the glasses by room temperature. Following one month the glasses need to appear to be identical and smell like short after the disinfecting. Besides, they should be a similar weight as in the past. One can free the cover a tad and smell the content if the Vermiculite stays at the ground.

In the event that there's a contamination, it makes it significantly simpler to determine its underlying foundations.

### 3.0 Inoculate and growth

The seeding of the spores is called immunize. Not grow through soil is likely to get infections. To avoid potential infections, utilize the following techniques:

### 3.1 One takes:

Inoculum (an ampulla or syringe for 10 glasses — this is for just for PF and PFE spores)

- ✓ Lighter
- ✓ Marker
- ✓ Needle
- ✓ Thermometer

## 3.2 Procedure

Close every window and entrance into your home (the bathrooms are perfect for this procedure). Wash everything with a combination of Spiritus and antibacterial cleanser.

(Plastic covered glass): Sit four holes in the cover with a hot needle inside the swivel. This is not important at the stage when you are using glasses for drinking. Use a four-hole cover as a guide here.

Shake the syringe with the intention that the spores scatter in the water and eliminate needle protection.

In a soot-free fire heat up the syringe tip. A switched shot glass with a drop of Spiritus out of a pipette is used for a soot-free fire. A drop absorbs the optimal amount of time, exactly.

Place a needle through an opening and let it cool down.

Take the syringe as a ring finger between the thumbs and middle-the latchkey pointer. Keep the needle to the mirror, so that the needle tip opening is clear.

During the time that the inoculum drops into the glass you need to take the finger out of the latchkey and sit tight at that point for about a second taking the needle back. In case the syringe clogs one withdraws the blockage and you dispose of it. Warning: Don't breathe into the gap!

Repeat the four to six levels until each opening is resistant. A while later, with the help of a soot-free fire, clean the needle again and put on the protection, so you can store the impenetrable syringe.

Seal a sellotape to the holes in the cover and write the date on the bottle.

If the spores in the main glass expand, vaccinate the following glass. In a month's time you can harvest along those lines for your own use. More time, space and material expense pointless, and can reduce the quality.

### 3.3 Sprinkling and growth

Place the glasses in a residue-free place with no sunlight within a temperature range of 15–30 degrees celsius. An excellent match for that is a cooler. You can use a lamp to sparkle from the glasses if heath is needed. Do not use heat from below as this dries the soil out. Within a week, there are small white stains rising on the Myzel, and Mycelia emerging through the soil in the second week.

### 4.0 Culture surroundings

When there are primordium rising up out of the soil you can remove the glass. (Be careful with not decimating the young shrooms!) Cut the parts which are not grown through with a hot blade out of the cake, so you don't get any infections. Just full grown through soils ought to be used for fructification as though this isn't the case the risk for infections is a lot higher.

## 4.1 Procedure

Turn over the glass and remove the cake carefully from it. If pieces are breaking of you can put it back and it will grow on once more. The cake will smell severely and remembers to the smell of harvest time leaves. Be careful in the event that it smells somewhat sharp or smelly. Remove drops with toilette paper. Ordinarily, harmed cakes do have recolors on it, yet this isn't associated with the process of disintegrate.

## 4.2 Culture environment

In a good culture form:

The relative humidity stays above 85%

Ventilation and temperature are effectively controllable

The cakes can be enlightened

Everything is easy to clean

### 4.2.1 One takes:

Small aquarium or a straightforward fruit bowl

Straightforward bag or Plexiglas table and cover

Positioned out (saturated with water) Perlit

Plant sprayer with high pressure

### 4.2.2 Construction and situating

If you don't mind see the drawings for the development. In a bag with just one cake, the modesty stays high, you won't get any contamination and you'll have oxygen shortage. For the pressing of a few cakes are advantages and disadvantages the specific inverse. Perlit is capillary and lets water disintegrate speedier than Vermiculite. Add the required Perlit while it is cooking. The fume will deal with the quick humidification of the form. At that point put in the small aquarium or the fruit bowl into the bag and afterward close it. Put or attach the bag into an ice chest. Attach a black light over it. Be careful and make sure that there is enough separation between the bag and the black light, so the cake won't get dried out. Neither the black light nor the bureau is really essential — you'd likewise have the option to attach the bag in a tent or at a tree.

### 4.3 Nebulize process

Nebulize routinely at regular intervals the air with water. The haze will add fresh oxygen and will break down azotic. Shrooms are protected against direct water drops, so you don't have to stress over that one. Excess water can be driven away through a whole on the bottom.

### 4.4 Light, air and temperature

Most primordien will grow in light of 370 nanometer (beautification blacklight). Shrooms will grow to the light. Be that as it may, a photo time of beyond what 12 hours can be harmful to the shrooms.

The intensity of the light isn't that important. In the event that you despite everything can peruse with this light that is sufficiently fair. Every day ventilation is recommended. Too much carbon dioxide will hinder the growth of the hut of a few shroom species. With Psilocybe cubensis this won't be a big issue, however. The shrooms are growing with at the fastest speed when you create an environment with around 30-degree celsius. In any case, they won't be that potent nor solid. From the earliest starting point of working of some shroom pre-states a temperature of 21-degree celsius is preferably.

### 4.5 Shrooms and malformation

The primordial shroom rises out of the small white dots which will turn into yellow little shrooms. The first ones are deformed and will stop growing in just a few days.

The tip of an infant shroom that is "outbound" will get black gray, later black and deform from round to irregular. The hut is going to fall prematurely and get particularly thick. Various malformations exist as white knobs. Before they become brittle, harvest them with a needle-malformations, are extremely powerful!

From other pre-states the customary shrooms expand. Harvesting a quarter of the weight of the wet soil is pretty much normal. There were 4 yields of up to 60 percent in excellent situations.

5.0 Inoculum raising shroom mature spores discolor the dark cake. The danger of contamination occurs during the preparation of the inoculum. So, make sure that you function properly.

### 5.1 One takes:

✓ Glass with cover made out of steal
✓ Foil

- ✓ Pot or oven
- ✓ Spiritus
- ✓ Suds
- ✓ Bended cuticle scissors
- ✓ Small knife
- ✓ Lighter
- ✓ Cotton fleece
- ✓ Shot glass

### 5.1.1 Procedure

Tinfoil to protect the glass and possibly a flexible unit. Placed the cover in a mixture of spirits and suds by then.

Put the glasses into the broiler at 150-degree celsius for about thirty minutes or cook them out in a closed oven. The glass must not have contact to the bottom in a jar.

The windows and gateways are locked. Wash the dividers and use suds / spiritus utensils.

Placed the cooled glass alongside the cake with sporulating shrooms on the right side. Place the turned cover on the right side as well. Place a rotating shot glass with some spirit (70–80 percent) on the left side of the cake. Also put the lighter by it.

Free the foil, so you can remove it from the glass with one hand.

Douse a spirit ball made of cotton. You cleanse the knife and the scissor with this.

Light on spirit at shot glass at the edge. Steam the scissor and the tip of the knife.

Sting the hut with the knife and with the scissor pick off the stem.

Do not hold your hands over the glass — pull the foil away — cut the hut out of the knife with the scissor (see drawing nr. 10) and then put it into the glass that you can open as of now.

Let the glass rest at room temperature for 4 days.

Remove a hot knife from the hut and let the spore engrave dry. For a year, that one should be storable.

### 5.2 Production of the inoculum

Cook a syringe and a glass of water with a hidden entire in the cover for an hour long in a pot stacked up with water. Sting an opening into the cover of the glass where the spore engrave is put away. Sterilize the needle by heating and inject a touch of cooled and sterile water over the spores. Stick the opening with the objective that it's close again and freeze the spore water. Defrost it from there on in a manner so the glass stands inclined. While doing this, manage the ice squares. The water must not contact the cover at whatever point. Make sure the glass is hermetically sealed.

### 5.3 Filling of the syringes

Take a pot and fill it with water. By then cook a syringe in it similarly as a glass stacked up with water which has a hidden opening in the cover. This you time for about an hour. Sterilize the needle by heating and inject a layer of cooled and sterile water into the glass with the spore water. Hold the glass inclined and pull the syringe totally. Sterilize the needle by heating again and pack the syringe water/air proof.

## 6.0 Harvesting and conservation

Young shrooms are better than old ones.

Note: Decide for each shroom whether you sporulate it, eat it or if you have to dispose of it. Don't store the shrooms: the fresher the shrooms are the more potent they will be.

### 6.1 Harvesting

Affecting substances will amass themselves in the huts of the young shrooms. At the point when the sporulating procedure begins the shrooms will lose step by step of their potency. The snapshot of harvesting for devouring is then legitimate, when the assurance fleece is opening.

### 6.1.1 Once takes:

- ✓ Dry hands
- ✓ Sharp knife
- ✓ Needle

### 6.1.2 Procedure

Reap with dry hands. Push the shroom with a pivoting improvement away from the cake. Utilize a needle for the shorter ones. Cut social occasions of adnate shrooms first and thereafter remove the stumps.

### 6.2 Conservation

Blue shading shows oxidation of the Psilocybin. UV light, humidity, warmth and oxygen quicken this procedure. Drying and enemies of oxidants will obstruct this particular procedure.

## 6.3 Drying

Drying will decrease stomach and gut distress. Dried shrooms are best for limit.

### 6.3.1 One takes:

- ✓  15-watt bulb
- ✓  Thermometer
- ✓  Shirt or sheets
- ✓  Box
- ✓  Pin

### 6.3.2 Procedure

Cut holes in the sides of the box and place the bulb some place in it. Stretch the shirt or sheet as a shade over it and fix it. Put the shrooms and the thermometer on it. Make sure that the temperature won't outperform 30-degree celsius. When the shrooms begin to get wrinkled remove the Vermiculite. New shrooms then can be put away impermeable and without humidity in the cooler.

# CHAPTER 13

## *Legal status of psilocybin mushrooms*

The legal status of illegal actions involving psilocybin mushrooms varies throughout the world. Under the 1971 United Nations Convention on Psychotropic Substances, psilocybin and psilocin are listed as Schedule I drugs. Schedule I drugs are defined as drugs with high potential for abuse or drugs that have no recognized medical uses. Psilocybin mushrooms, however, have had numerous medicinal and religious uses throughout history in dozens of cultures, and have significantly lower potential for abuse than other Schedule I drugs.

U.N. treaties do not regulate psilocybin mushrooms. From a letter to the Dutch Ministry of Health, dated 13 September 2001, from Herbert Schaepe, Chairman of the United Nations International Narcotics Control Board.

As you know, mushrooms containing the aforementioned substances are collected and used for their hallucinogens. As a matter of international law, under the 1971 Convention on Psychotropic Substances, no plants (natural material) containing Psilocybe and psilocybin are currently under jurisdiction. Preparations made of these plants are therefore not subject to international control and, therefore, are not subject to the articles of the 1971 Convention. Criminal cases are decided with respect to domestic law, which might otherwise provide for restrictions on psilocybin and psilocybin-containing mushrooms. Since the Board can only speak about the contours of the international drug conventions, I cannot give an opinion on the litigation at issue.

However, many countries have some level of psilocybin mushroom regulation or prohibition (for example, the US Psychotropic Substances Act, the UK Misuse of Drugs Act 1971, and the Canadian Controlled Drugs and Substances Act). The ban on psilocybin mushrooms has been criticized by the general public and by researchers who see therapeutic potential in drug addictions and other mental instabilities such as PTSD, anxiety and depression. There are also relatively few medical risks among regulated drugs, psilocybin mushrooms.

There is a lot of ambiguity about the legal status of psilocybin mushrooms in many national, state, and provincial drug laws, as well as a strong element of selective enforcement in some places, since psilocybin and psilocin are considered illegal to possess as substances without a license, but mushrooms themselves are not mentioned in those laws. The legal status of Psilocybe spores is even more ambiguous, as the spores do not contain either psilocybin or psilocin, and thus are not illegal to sell or possess in many jurisdictions, although many jurisdictions will prosecute items used in drug manufacturing under broader laws. A few jurisdictions (such as Georgia and Idaho, the US states) have specifically banned the sale and possession of psilocybin mushroom spores. Psilocybin mushroom production is considered drug manufacturing in most jurisdictions and is often heavily penalized, though some countries and one US state have ruled that growing psilocybin mushrooms do not qualify as a controlled substance "manufacturing."

### Steps to Mushroom Farming

Mushroom cultivating comprises of six stages, and despite the fact that the divisions are to some degree arbitrary, these means distinguish what is expected to form a creation system.

The six stages of mushroom cultivating:

### Stage I

1. Composting

### Stage II

2. Composting

3. Spawning

4. Casing

5. Sticking

6. Editing

These means are described in their naturally occurring arrangement, stressing the notable features within each progression. Compost gives supplements expected to mushroom to grow. Two types of material are generally used for mushroom compost, the most used and most affordable being wheat straw-bedded horse manure. Synthetic compost is generally made from roughage and squashed corncobs, in spite of the fact that the term often alludes to any mushroom compost where the prime fixing isn't horse manure. The two types of compost require the addition of nitrogen supplements and a molding specialist, gypsum.

The preparation of compost occurs in two stages alluded to as Phase I and Phase II composting. The discussion of compost preparation and mushroom creation begins with Phase I composting.

**Stage I:**

**1. Making Mushroom Compost**

This period of compost preparation as a rule occurs outside albeit an enclosed structure or a structure with a rooftop over it might be used. A solid section, alluded to as a wharf, is needed for composting. Also, a compost turner to aerate and water the fixings, and a tractor-loader to move the fixings to the turner is required. In prior days heaps were turned by hand utilizing pitchforks, which is as yet an option in contrast to automated hardware, however it is work intensive and truly requesting.

Stage I composting is started by mixing and wetting the fixings as they are stacked in a rectangular heap with tight sides and a free center. Typically, the mass fixings are put through a compost turner. Water can be sprayed onto the horse manure or synthetic compost as these materials travel through the turner. Nitrogen enhancements and gypsum are spread over the top of the mass fixings and are completely mixed by the turner. When the heap is wetted and formed, high-impact aging (composting) commences because of the growth and multiplication of microorganisms, which occur naturally in the mass fixings. Heat, smelling salts, and carbon dioxide are discharged as side-effects during this process. Compost activators, other than those referenced, are not required, albeit some natural cultivating books pressure the requirement for an "activator."

Mushroom compost creates as the chemical idea of the raw fixings is changed over by the activity of microorganisms, heat, and some heat-discharging chemical reactions. These occasions bring about a food source generally appropriate for the growth of the mushroom to the rejection of other fungi and bacteria. There must be sufficient moisture, oxygen, nitrogen, and carbohydrates present all through the process, or else the process will stop. This is the reason water and enhancements are added occasionally, and the compost heap is aerated as it travels through the turner.

Gypsum is added to limit the oiliness compost ordinarily tends to have. Gypsum expands the flocculation of specific chemicals in the compost, and they cling to straw or roughage as opposed to filling the pores (holes) between the straws. A side advantage of this phenomenon is that air can permeate the heap all the more readily, and air is essential to the composting process. The prohibition of air results in an airless (anaerobic) environment in which pernicious chemical mixes are formed which bring down the selectivity of mushroom compost for cultivating mushrooms. Gypsum is added at the outset of composting at 40 pounds per ton of dry fixings.

Nitrogen supplements in general use today incorporate brewer's grain, seed meals of soybeans, peanuts, or cotton, and chicken manure, among others. The purpose of these enhancements is to expand the nitrogen content to 1.5 percent for horse manure or 1.7 percent for synthetic, both computed on a dry weight premise. Synthetic compost requires the addition of urea or ammonium nitrate at the outset of composting to give the compost microflora a readily accessible form of nitrogen for their growth and multiplication.

Corn cobs are sometimes inaccessible or accessible at a price considered to be unnecessary. Substitutes for or supplements to corn cobs incorporate destroyed hardwood bark, cottonseed hulls, killed grape pomace, and cocoa bean hulls. The executives of a compost heap containing any of these materials is novel in the requirements for watering and the interim between turnings.

The underlying compost heap ought to be 5 to 6 feet wide, 5 to 6 feet high, and as long as essential. A two-sided box can be used to form the heap (rick), albeit a few turners are outfitted with a "ricker", so a box isn't required. The sides of the heap ought to be firm and thick, yet the center must remain free all through Phase I composting. As the straw or feed softens during composting, the materials become less inflexible and compactions can without much of a stretch occur. If the materials become excessively conservative, air can't travel through the heap and an anaerobic environment will create.

Turning and watering are done at approximately 2-day interims, yet not except if the heap is hot (145° to 170°F). Turning gives the chance to water, aerate, and mix the fixings, just as to move the straw or feed from a cooler to a warmer area in the heap, outside versus inside. Enhancements are likewise added when the ricks are turned, however they ought to be added early in the composting process. The number of turnings and the time between turnings depends on the state of the starting material and the time fundamental for the compost to heat to temperatures above 145°F.

### Steps to Mushroom Farming

Mushroom cultivating comprises of six stages, and despite the fact that the divisions are to some degree arbitrary, these means recognize what is expected to form a creation system.

### The six stages of mushroom cultivating

1. Composting
2. Composting
3. Spawning
4. Casing

5. Sticking

6. Trimming

These means are described in their naturally occurring succession, accentuating the remarkable features within each progression. Compost gives supplements expected to mushroom to grow. Two types of material are generally used for mushroom compost, the most utilized and most affordable being wheat straw-bedded horse manure. Synthetic compost is generally made from feed and squashed corncobs, despite the fact that the term often alludes to any mushroom compost where the prime fixing isn't horse manure. The two types of compost require the addition of nitrogen supplements and a molding operator, gypsum.

The preparation of compost occurs in two stages alluded to as Phase I and Phase II composting. The discussion of compost preparation and mushroom creation begins with Phase I composting.

## Stage I

### 1. Making Mushroom Compost

This period of compost preparation typically occurs outside albeit an enclosed structure or a structure with a rooftop over it might be used. A solid section, alluded to as a wharf, is required for composting. Also, a compost turner to aerate and water the fixings, and a tractor-loader to move the fixings to the turner is required. In prior days heaps were turned by hand utilizing pitchforks, which is as yet an option in contrast to automated gear, yet it is work intensive and truly requesting.

Stage I composting is started by mixing and wetting the fixings as they are stacked in a rectangular heap with tight sides and a free center. Regularly, the mass fixings are put through a compost turner. Water is sprinkled onto the horse manure or synthetic compost as these materials travel through the turner. Nitrogen enhancements and gypsum are spread over the top of the mass fixings and are completely mixed by the turner. When the heap is wetted and formed, vigorous maturation (composting) commences because of the growth and proliferation of microorganisms, which occur naturally in the mass fixings. Heat, smelling salts, and carbon dioxide are discharged as results during this process. Compost activators, other than those referenced, are not required, albeit some natural cultivating books pressure the requirement for an "activator."

Mushroom compost creates as the chemical idea of the raw fixings is changed over by the activity of microorganisms, heat, and some heat-discharging chemical reactions. These occasions bring about a food source generally appropriate for the growth of the mushroom to the rejection of other fungi and bacteria. There must be satisfactory moisture, oxygen, nitrogen, and carbohydrates present all through the process, or else the process will stop. This is the reason water and enhancements are added occasionally, and the compost heap is aerated as it travels through the turner.

Gypsum is added to limit the oiliness compost ordinarily tends to have. Gypsum expands the flocculation of specific chemicals in the compost, and they hold fast to straw or feed instead of filling the pores (holes) between the straws. A side advantage of this phenomenon is that air can permeate the heap all the more readily, and air is essential to the composting process. The rejection of air results in an airless (anaerobic) environment in which malicious chemical mixes are formed which take away from the selectivity of mushroom compost for growing mushrooms. Gypsum is included at the outset of composting at 40 lbs. per ton of dry fixings.

Nitrogen supplements in general use today incorporate brewer's grain, seed meals of soybeans, peanuts, or cotton, and chicken manure, among others. The purpose of these enhancements is to build the nitrogen content to 1.5 percent for horse manure or 1.7 percent for synthetic, both computed on a dry weight premise. Synthetic compost requires the addition of ammonium nitrate or urea at the outset of composting to give the compost microflora a readily accessible form of nitrogen for their growth and proliferation.

Corn cobs are sometimes inaccessible or accessible at a price considered to be extreme. Substitutes for or supplements to corn cobs incorporate destroyed hardwood bark, cottonseed hulls, killed grape pomace, and cocoa bean hulls. The board of a compost heap containing any of these materials is remarkable in the requirements for watering and the interim between turnings.

The underlying compost heap ought to be 5 to 6 feet wide, 5 to 6 feet high, and as long as essential. A two-sided box can be utilized to form the heap (rick), albeit a few turners are furnished with a "ricker", so a box isn't required. The sides of the heap ought to be firm and thick, yet the center must remain free all through Phase I composting. As the straw or roughage softens during composting, the materials become less inflexible and compactions can without much of a stretch occur. In the event that the materials become excessively smaller, air can't travel through the heap and an anaerobic environment will create.

Turning and watering is done at intervals of about 2 days, but not except when the heap is hot (145 ° to 170 ° F). Turning gives the opportunity to wash, aerate and mix the fixings, just as it helps the straw or feed to move from a cooler to a warmer place in the heap, outside versus inside. Equally, changes are applied when the ricks are turned, but should be added early in the composting process. The number of turns and the time between turns depends on the state of the starting material and the fundamental time to heat up to temperatures above 145 ° F for the compost.

## 4. Casing

The casing is a top-dressing added to the spawn-run compost that ultimately shapes the mushrooms. Clay-topsoil field soil, a combination of peat moss with calcareous earth, or weathered recycled, spent compost can be used as a casing. Casing does not need to waste time with supplements because casing is a water store and a place where rhizomorphs are produced. Rhizomorphs tend to be thick strings, which develop when the very fine mycelium fuses.

Initials to the mushrooms, primordia, or pins appear on the rhizomorphs, so there will be no mushrooms without rhizomorphs. Case should be sanitized for the execution of any insects and pathogens which it may pass on. Similarly, it is important to spread the casing so that the depth is uniform over the compost surface. Such uniformity makes it possible for the spawn to pass in and through the casing at a similar rate, and eventually to produce mushrooms at the same time. Casing should have the option to retain moisture as moisture is central to a firm mushroom's growth.

Dealing with the yield in the case wake requires that the compost temperature be kept in the case wake at about 75 ° F for up to 5 days, and that the relative humidity should be high. From that point on, until small mushroom initials (pins) have grown, the compost temperature should be consistently reached down 2 ° F. Water has to be added intermittently throughout the period following the casing to raise the level of humidity to field efficiency before the mushroom pins shape. Understanding when, how and how much water to apply for casing is a "job of craftsmanship" that distinguishes seasoned growers from beginners readily.

## 5. Staying

Initials of the mushroom build after rhizomorphs develop in the casing. The initials on a rhizomorph are incredibly small and may be seen as outgrowths. The structure is a pin at a point where a secret quadruple in size. Through the catch arrangement pins continue to expand and grow larger, and ultimately a catch enlarges to a mushroom. Harvestable mushrooms in the wake of the casing appear to be 18 to 21 days. Pins are produced by bringing fresh air into the growing room when the carbon dioxide content of room air is reduced to 0.08 per cent or lower, depending on the cultivar. Outside air is about 0.04 percent containing carbon dioxide.

The arranging of fresh air presentation is important and is something adapted interestingly through experience. Generally, it is ideal to ventilate as small as possible until the mycelium has started to show up at the surface of the casing, and to stop watering when pin initials are forming. If the carbon dioxide is cut down too early by means of airing too soon, the mycelium stops growing through the casing and mushroom initials form beneath the surface of the casing. Everything considered mushrooms continue growing, they push through the casing and are dirty at harvest time. Too little moisture can likewise bring about mushrooms forming beneath the surface of the casing. Staying influences both the potential yield and nature of a harvest and is a colossal development in the creation cycle.

## 6. Trimming

The terms flush, break, or blossom are names given to the repeating 3-to 5-day harvest periods during the trimming cycle; these are followed by several days when no mushrooms are available to harvest. This cycle repeats itself in a musical way, and harvesting can go on as long as mushrooms continue maturing. Most mushroom farmers harvest for 35 to 42 days, yet some harvest a yield for 60 days, and harvest can proceed for as long as 150 days.

For good results, the air temperature should be kept between 57 ° to 62 ° F during trimming. This temperature range favors mushroom growth, but cooler temperatures will protract both disease pathogens and insect bugs from life examples. It can give the impression of being strange that there are threats that can damage mushrooms, no harvest that doesn't have to deal with different species is grown anyway. Aggravation of the mushroom can cause total yield failures, and often the critical factor in how far a harvest is dependent on the extent of infiltration of the vermin. Cultural practices combined with the use of pesticides will control these pests and insects, however it is usually appealing to exclude these species from the rising rooms.

The relative humidity in the growing rooms should be sufficiently high to limit the drying of the casing anyway not too high to cause clammy or tenacious to the cap surfaces of creating mushrooms. Water is added to the casing to prevent water pressure from producing mushrooms; this means watering 2 to 3 times a week in business practice. Every watering may include quite a lot of gallons, depending on the dryness of the wrapper, the cultivar being grown, and the time of the pins, buttons, or mushrooms going forward. The majority of first-time growers add a lot of water and the surface of the case seals; this is seen as a lack of texture on the casing sheet. Sealed case prevents the exchange of gases which are necessary for the formation of mushroom pins. One can measure how much water has been harvested after the first break by remembering that 90 per cent of the mushroom is water and a gallon of water weight 8.3 lbs. Where 100 lbs. 90 lbs of mushrooms have been picked. Water has been removed from the casing; and this is the thing to replace before the second break creates mushrooms.

Outdoor air is used to monitor the temperatures of both air and compost during the outline of harvest time. The carbon dioxide given off by the rising mycelium is also replaced by outdoor air. The more mycelial growth, the more carbon dioxide produced, and since more growth occurs early in the yield, the more fresh air is required during the two breaks that underlie it. Likewise, the amount of fresh air depends on the growing mushrooms, the area of the distribution floor, the amount of compost provided in the growing room and the state or piece of fresh air. Experience is apparently the best guide on the volume of air required, but there is a general guideline: 0.3ft / hour when the compost is 8 inches deep, and 50 to 100 percent of this volume must be outside air.

A question often arises about the need for enlightenment while the mushrooms grow. Mushrooms do not need light to grow, photosynthesis requires light only from green plants. Growing rooms can be illuminated to promote harvesting or cropping activities, but it is more popular for staff or mushroom farmers to be furnished with miner's lamps instead of lighting a whole house.

Ventilation is important for growing mushrooms, and humidity and temperature controls are also required. A cold mist or live steam may add humidity to the air, or simply by wetting the walls and floors. Moisture can be removed from the growing room by: 1) allowing for a larger volume of outdoor air; 2) introducing drier air; 3) moving the same amount of outdoor air and heating it up to a higher temperature, as warmer air holds more moisture and thus lowers relative humidity. Control of temperature in a mushroom growing room is no different from control of temperature in your home. Heat can come from hot water that circulates through pipes that are mounted on walls. In recent mushroom farms, hot, forced air can be blown through a ventilation duct, which is rather common. There are a few mushroom farms in limestone caves where, depending on the time of year, the rock serves as both a heating and cooling surface. Caves of any kind are not necessarily suitable for growing mushrooms, and abandoned coal mines have too many intrinsic problems for a mushroom farm to be considered viable sites. Only calcareous caves require extensive reconstruction and enhancement before they are suitable for growing mushrooms, and only the growth occurs in the cave where composting takes place at a wharf above ground.

Mushrooms are harvested in a 7-to 10-day cycle, but this may be longer or shorter depending on the temperature, moisture, cultivar and the stage when they are picked. Once picking mature mushrooms a mushroom growth inhibitor is eliminated and the next flush progresses towards maturity. Mushrooms are usually picked at a time when the veil isn't stretched too far. Consumers in North America want mushrooms closed, tight, while flat mushrooms are wanted open in England and Australia. A mushroom's maturity is assessed by how far the veil is stretched, and not by how big the mushroom is. Consequently, mature mushrooms are both large and small, although both farmers and consumers prefer mushrooms of medium to large size.

Methods of picking and packaging also differ between farms. Freshly harvested mushrooms must be kept at 35 ° to 45 ° F for refrigeration. It is vital that mushrooms "breathe" after harvest to extend the shelf-life of the mushrooms, so storage in a non-waxed paper bag is preferred to a plastic bag.

The growing room should be closed off after the last flush of mushrooms has been collected, and the room should be pasteurized with steam. This final pasteurization is designed to destroy any pests that may be present in the growing room in the crop or woodwork, thereby minimizing the likelihood of infesting the next crop.

### Conclusion

It takes about 15 weeks to complete a complete production cycle, from the beginning of composting to the final steaming off after harvesting has finished. A mushroom grower should expect from 0 to 4 lbs. in any position for this job. The national average for 1980 was 3.12 lbs. per square foot; Every Foot Square. Final yield depends on how well a grower has controlled the temperature, humidity, pests, etc. All things considered, the most significant factors for good production appear to be experience plus an intuitive feel for the commercial mushroom's biological rhythms. After the fundamentals of mushroom growth are known, the production system used to grow a crop can be selected.

Made in United States
Troutdale, OR
01/18/2024